To the men and women of the counter.
May your customers be bathed,
and your parts always in stock.

Hello, Parts

How I started selling car parts and lost faith in humanity

JOSH WELLINGTON

[Table of Contents]

[About the author]

Josh Wellington's academic achievements are non-existent. He's a borderline competent writer, and the fact that he's managed to cobble this book together is something of a miracle. His only accolade is having once stood behind Will Ferrell at a Starbucks. He currently resides in a large, empty house in the suburbs of Chicago, where none of his neighbors have ever called the cops on him for mowing his lawn.

[Introduction]

Speaking entirely impartially, the people of the Parts Department are the unsung heroes of every car dealership. They are, by far, the smartest, hardest-working, best-looking people in the place, who love nothing more than picking up the messes of every other department in addition to their own work. Okay, that last bit was a lie, but the rest is 100% spot on.

What exactly is the Parts Department?

The Parts Department is an integral link in the overall Service Department of a car dealership. It typically consists of:

A Mechanics Counter, where our ~~grease-smeared wrench monkeys~~ smart and talented techs can ~~shout~~ politely request the parts that they need to ~~unfuck~~ fix customer vehicles in the shop.

A Retail Counter, where the ~~drooling, unwashed masses~~ general public can ~~shamble up and tell us how bad we are at our jobs~~ seek our expertise, even though they routinely know far more than we do, in finding and acquiring the parts they require for their own vehicles.

And a warehouse stocking thousands, or even tens of thousands of ~~haphazardly tossed~~ meticulously organized and cataloged parts for a variety of vehicles within the purview of the brands handled by the dealership. The warehouse also serves as a universal trash bin for anything that someone can't find a place for elsewhere in the building.

What follows is a glimpse into Parts' daily dealings with the public, both on the phones and at the counter. I can't stress this enough — these are actual interactions with real people.

Note on VINs -

Your car's Vehicle Identification Number, or VIN, is the car's unique serial number. With either the whole VIN, or a portion (like the last 8 digits), the parts catalog can filter all of the specific options of your vehicle, which helps to ensure you get the correct parts. If you want Parts to love you, ALWAYS have your VIN handy.

[Chapter 1]

Hello, Parts

Me: *Hello, Parts.*

Customer: **You guys sell Ford parts, right?**

Me: *Nope, this is a Chevrolet Dealership.*

Customer: **Oh, so if I needed to get like a fender part for a Ford, you guys wouldn't have that?**

Me: *Nope, we only sell parts for General Motors vehicles.*

Customer: **Oh, who should I call to get parts then?**

Me: *I would recommend calling a Ford dealership.*

Customer: **Oh, well that makes sense.**

[Evidently, it's not common knowledge that these are different companies.]

Me: *Hello, Parts.*

Customer: **Yeah, where y'all located?**

Me: *[Gives local cross streets]*

Customer: **No, I meant in the building!**

Me: *Oh... uh... Next to the cashier?*

Customer: **Alright, I'm gonna come and see you.**

[He was in the showroom... of course...]

Me: *Hello, Parts.*

Customer: **Yes, I was wondering if you could tell me what kind of car I have.**

Me: *Uhhh... I guess... What does it say on the back?*

Customer: **It says Saturn, but I don't think that's what it is.**

Me: *Yeah... What's the VIN number?*

Customer: **[Gives VIN number]**

Me: *Okay, that's a Saturn SL-2.*

Customer: **Alright, whatever you say.**

[It was very clear that he still didn't believe me.]

Me: *Hello, Parts.*

Customer: **I got a 2006 Impala. S... S. and I need that little round hoopdie up on the front.**

Me: *... What?*

Customer: **On the front of the engine, it's got 5 bolts.**

Me: *... The... water pump?*

Customer: **Yeah, that's the one. I need one of them.**

[One of my better random guesses.]

[At the counter]

Me: *Hi, can I help you?*

Customer: **I need that box on the transmission.**

Me: *Alright, which box are we talking about? Do you know what it's called?*

Customer: **No.**

Me: *Okay, do you know what it does?*

Customer: **No.**

Me: *Do you know what it's connected to?*

Customer: **No. But I know I broke it.**

[And somehow still more prepared than most people that walked up to the counter.]

[At the counter]

Me: *Hi, is there something I can help you with?*

Customer: **Yeah, I got a '94 Camaro, and I need that L-shaped pipe.   Here, I got a picture.**

            [Shows picture on his phone]

Me: *Sir, there are no L-shaped pipes in this picture.*

Customer: **I know, but there's s'posed to be.**

[He was genuinely confused that his picture of nothing didn't help me.]

Me: *Hello, Parts.*

Customer: **Hi, my name is Olan. I bought a car and it needs tires.**

Me: *Oookay... What size tires are you looking for?*

Customer: **Mine has 54,000 miles.**

Me: *Alright, but what size tire are you looking for?*

Customer: **My name is Olan.**

Me: *Okay, but what size tires are you looking for?*

Customer: **Oh, you need to know what size they are? I don't know. Just give me a price on anything.**

Me: *Uhhhh... Okay. $1000 per tire.*

Customer: **Man, you crazy. [Hangs up]**

[Yes... I am the crazy one...]

Me: *Hello, Parts.*

Customer: **I need a manual.**

Me: *... Uh, okay, for what sort of car?*

Customer: **Chevy.**

Me: *... Okay... What sort of Chevy?*

Customer: **'94.**

Me: *Alright... Chevrolet had quite a few models in 1994, could we be slightly more specific?*

Customer: **I just said, it's a '94 Chevy. I need a manual.**

Me: *... ... Uhh... That's discontinued.*

Customer: **Man, whatever. [Hangs up]**

[When in doubt, say it's discontinued.]

Me: *Hello, Parts.*

Customer: **I need to get some of them special handles.**

Me: *Alright, what sort of car are we looking at?*

Customer: **It's a '12 Impala.**

Me: *And we're looking for... special handles?*

Customer: **Yeah, I want them special lookin' ones.**

Me: *...Special handles... Chrome?*

Customer: **Are those the ones that makes the car look special?**

Me: *Yeah, I suppose they do.*

Customer: **Then I want to get some of those.**

Me: *Hello, Parts.*

Customer: **Oh, you are open today.**

Me: *Clearly.*

Customer: **[Hangs up]**

[This call happened surprisingly often.]

[At the counter]

Customer: **I need some of these.**
[Drops something on the counter]

Me: *Ummm, alright...That's an interesting looking... clip? I haven't really seen anything like that before; what's it for?*

Customer: **Vertical blinds.**

Me: *... ...As in, for your house?*

Customer: **Yeah, he told me I could come up here and get some.**

Me: *For vertical blinds? No, I'm sorry, this is a Chevrolet dealership, we don't sell parts for vertical blinds.*

Customer: **I wanna talk to your manager.**

Me: *He'll be in on Monday, but he doesn't sell parts for vertical blinds either.*

[One day I'd like to meet this mysterious "He."]

Me: *Hello, Parts.*

Customer: **Man, gimme one of them squirters.**

Me: *... ... What?*

Customer: **My car needs a new squirter.**

Me: *... ... Okay. What kind of car do you have?*

Customer: **'02 Impala.**

Me: *And you're looking for a washer nozzle?*

Customer: **Naw man, I don't need the nozzle, I need the squirter.**

Me: *Aren't those the same thing?*

Customer: **Naw man, the nozzle is that part that sprays on your windshield. The *squirter* is that part that sprays on your windshield.**

Me: *... Okay, yeah, I'm really confused now.*

Customer: **Man, I'll just call someone else.**

[He eventually came in... and bought a washer nozzle...]

[At the counter]

Customer: **I need to get one of these over here. [Points to a hat in the display case]**

Me: *Absolutely, let me get that for you. [Grabs it from the case and gives it to him]*

Customer: **Alright, well, how do I?... How do I?... [Looking at the hat]**

Me: *How do you... what? It's a hat... you just put it on your head.*

Customer: **Oooh. Alright.**

[This man was wearing a hat, so I figured he was familiar with the general concept of how they worked... teach me to make assumptions.]

Me: *Hello, Parts.*

Customer: **Hi, I need a lower Pentium intake port.
               You all know what that is?**

Me: *Nope.*

Customer: **Either do I. I'll call you back.**

[This level of self-awareness did not come along often enough.]

[At the counter]

Me: *Hi, can I help you?*

Customer: **I need control arm bolts for a '03 Tahoe.**

Me: *Alright, let me check. Yeah, we have those, they're $3.60 each.*

Customer: **Gimme two.**

Me: *You got it. One sec.*
             [Brings the bolts to the counter]

Customer: **Well where are the nuts?**

Me: *You... didn't ask for nuts.*

Customer: **I know I didn't ask for 'em, but you shoulda brought 'em anyhow.**

[How silly of me, only bringing you the thing... that you asked for.]

[At the counter]

Me: *Hi, is there something I can help you with?*

Customer: **Yeah, you can get me the parts guy.**

              [Long pause]

Me: *Yeah, that's me.*

Customer: **Oh.**

[In his defense, I was standing behind a counter with a large "Parts" sign next to it; I could have been literally anyone.]

Me: *Hello, Parts.*

Customer: **Is it too late to get two of 'em?**

Me: *Ummmm... What?*

Customer: **Tires, I need tires for my car!**

Me: *Okay... What size tires are you looking for?*

Customer: **Ohhhhh, lord have mercy, I don't know.**

Me: *Well, what kind of car do you have?*

Customer: **It's a 708.**

Me: *Yeah, that's not a car.*

Customer: **Oh, Jesus Christ.**

[Every time I picked up the phone, and there was a person on the other end looking for tires, I died a little on the inside.]

Me: *Hello, Parts.*

Customer: **Yeah man, I got a 2003 Grand Prix, and I need that cooling line for the power steering.**

Me: *Alright, no problem. Do you have your VIN handy?*

Customer: **I got it, but it ain't gonna do you no good, because I put a whole different engine up in there.**

Me: *... Okay, well, unfortunately I'm not going to be able to look up anything for that...*

Customer: **Man, why not? It still says Grand Prix on it, so it's a Grand Prix.**

Me: *... Did you put a Grand Prix engine in it?*

Customer: **No man, why would I do that?**

Me: *Exactly.*

Me: *Hello, Parts.*

Customer: **Yeah man, I need a bumper, a fender, a headlight, a windshield, and a whole lotta emblems.**

Me: *... ... ... For what car?*

Customer: **For *my* car.**

Me: *Of course. See, I don't know you, or what kind of car you drive, so that doesn't really help me.*

Customer: **Well you asked what car it was for and I told you.**

[How silly of me.]

28

[At the counter]

Customer: **I need trans lines for my truck.**

Me: *Okay, what sort of truck do you have?*

Customer: **'08.**

Me: *... Okay... But what model is it?*

Customer: **You know, that little one, with the four doors.**

Me: *... Uhhhhhh... Alright. What is it called? What does it say on the back?*

Customer: **It's a Malibu.**

Me: *So it's not a truck, it's a car.*

Customer: **Nah, it's a truck. I need trans lines. I don't pay tax.**

Me: *That's getting a bit ahead, I'm still not sure we've even established what sort of car you have.*

Customer: **It's a truck.**

[I guess it could have been an El Camalibu...]

Me: *Hello, Parts.*

Customer: **Is my car four wheel drive?**

Me: *I don't know. What kind of car to you have? Or would you happen to have the VIN?*

Customer: **I don't need to tell you all that! I just need to know if it's four wheel drive!**

Me: *Well, unless you give me some more information, there's no way for me to tell you.*

Customer: **I'll just bring it into Service! They'll be able to tell me!**

[I should have just said yes...]

Me: *Hello, Parts.*

Customer: **Yeah... ... ...**

Me: *... ...*

Customer: **Um...I need that part...uh...yeah...ummm... ... that part... uhhh...**

Me: *Yes, what sort of part?*

Customer: **I need that part... where you pull your car in and they tell you what's wrong with it...**

Me: *The Service Department?*

Customer: **Yeah... I... want one of them.**

Me: *Hello, Parts.*

Customer: **I need a... a... turn signal lens... for a... a... '07 QX56.**

Me: *An Infiniti?*

Customer: **Yeah.**

Me: *This a Chevrolet dealership.*

Customer: **So you all don't have one?**

Me: *... No, you have to call Infiniti or Nissan.*

Customer: **[Hangs up]**

[Honestly, are people really not aware that these are different companies?]

Me: *Hello, Parts.*

Customer: **Yeah, do you all sell parts for Camaros? I got a 2012 and my mechanic said I need a part, but I don't know what the part is. You all got one?**

Me: *... Well... uh... What part are you looking for?*

Customer: **I just said I don't know.**

Me: *... ... Alright, well... I'm not sure I can help you.*

[How did you think this conversation was going to go?]

[Uhhh... Say what?]

"Hi, do you all have that beep boop boop beep that un-locks my car doors?"

"Ohhhhh, so I gotta know what kind of part I'm looking for in order for you to look it up?"

"I don't know what it is, but when I put my hand on it, it clicks. Do you have one of those?"

"Yeah man, I opened my hood this morning, and that piece that holds it up... It. Ain't. Doin'. Shit. And fuck that. You got one of those?"

[Chapter 2]

Hope Has Been Discontinued

Me: *Hello, Parts.*

Customer: **I got a '06 Malibu, and I need the trans fluid cap. I just broke mine.**

Me: *I believe the cap is actually the trans dipstick itself. It should be a little yellow handle in the front center of the engine.*

Customer: **No, man, my trans filler is up on top. It's got a big black cap on it.**

Me: *Hmmm, would you happen to still have the cap? Does it say anything on it, or have any symbols?*

Customer: **Yeah, I got it right here. It's got a picture of a steering wheel on it.**

Me: *Yeah, that's for your power steering fluid reservoir.*

Customer: **So that's not where I'm supposed to put my transmission fluid?**

Me: *Nope.*

[In his defense, the steering wheel is the universal symbol for transmission... right?]

Me: *Hello, Parts.*

Customer: **Hi, I received a call this morning saying that my parts were in.**

Me: *Okay.*

Customer: **So are my parts in?**

Me: *Yes, that's why you were called.*

[This call happened multiple times every day.]

[At the counter]

Customer: **Where was this part made? I don't want anything made in China.**

Me: *I have no clue, GM sources their parts from a variety of manufacturers around the world.*

Customer: **Well, it says Detroit right here.**

Me: *Yes, that's the location of GM headquarters.*

Customer: **Well, it says Kalamazoo right here.**

Me: *That's where the cardboard box was made.*

Customer: **Well, what if I buy and it's from China?**

Me: *Literally nothing will happen. A majority of your car is built from parts produced outside of the United States.*

Customer: **Oh, well I'm not okay with that.**

[Wish I was there when they looked at the bag and saw it was made in Mexico.]

Me: *Hello, Parts.*

Customer: **Yeah... what kinda tires go on a Cadillac?**

Me: *... Uhh, what sort of Cadillac do you have?*

Customer: **Deville.**

Me: *Okay... What year? And do you know what size tire you're looking for?*

Customer: **Nope, all I know is that they're black.**

[Well at least that rules out all of the other colors of tires we usually sell...]

Me: *Hello, Parts.*

Customer: **The '08 Cobalt's got a recall on it, and I gotta get my recall.**

Me: *Alright, well that's something that you'll have to speak to Service about. I can transfer you over to them if you'd like.*

Customer: **What if I don't have the car any more?**

Me: *Then the recall shouldn't concern you.*

[How would you even bring in the car to get the recall done?]

Me: *Hello, Parts.*

Customer: **Yeah, how much does it cost to get a battery for the chirps?**

Me: *Pardon me?*

Customer: **I need a battery for my chirps.**

Me: *Chirps? I have no idea what we're talking about right now.*

Customer: **You know, the chirps; the little thing with the buttons that unlocks my car.**

Me: *You mean a... remote?*

Customer: **Ohhhh, is that what you call them?!**

[There were three other people after this guy who used the term "chirps."]

Me: *Hello, Parts.*

Customer: **YOU HAVE DIPSTICKS IN STOCK?!**

Me: *Um... yes? It kinda depends on what sort of car you have...*

Customer: **IT'S 3 FEET LONG!**

Me: *I see. What kind of car do you have?*

Customer: **IT'S GOTTA GO ALL THE WAY DOWN IN THE ENGINE.**

Me: *Yes... I understand... But you still haven't told me what kind of car it's for.*

Customer: **TRUCK.**

Me: *Okay... What sort of truck is it for?*

Customer: **I DON'T KNOW! I JUST GOTTA COME GET ONE.**

[Yelling is a valid replacement for knowing what you're talking about.]

Me: *Hello, Parts.*

Customer: **Good morning. I'm looking for an upper trans line.**

Me: *... Okay, what sort of car do you have?*

Customer: **Hmmmmm, it's a 2003 Pontiac... Buick... Pontiac.**

Me: *Um, alright... What sort of car do you have?*

Customer: **It's a Pon... Bui... Pontiac!**

Me: *Alright, what model of Pontiac?*

Customer: **Did they make any cars that started with a "B" in 2003?**

Me: *They made the Bonneville.*

Customer: **Yeah! I have one of those!**

[It was wild how often people didn't know what sort of car they owned.]

[At the counter]

Me: *Hi, is there something I can help you with?*

Customer: **Yeah, you all need to sell me something to make my car louder.**

Me: *Louder?*

Customer: **Yeah, it's too quiet... and the ladies, they can't hear it none.**

[This guy is my hero.]

Me: *Hello, Parts.*

Customer: **My name's Alan, and I got a '01 Chevy, and my door don't close right. You got one of those?**

Me: *Do I... have... a door that doesn't close properly?*

Customer: **No, I need that part. I ordered parts from you before, my name is Alan.**

Me: *Okay... I have no idea what part we're talking about, and I still don't even know what kind of car you have.*

Customer: **I said it's a '01 Chevy.**

Me: *Chevrolet made a variety of vehicles in 2001, could we be slightly more specific?*

Customer: **Truck.**

Me: ...

[Chevy needs to make a vehicle that's just called "Truck". No options, no different models, it's just a "Truck." And they will all be exactly the same.]

Me: *Hello, Parts.*

Customer: **How much are Corvette emblems?**

Me: *Well, it kinda varies by which emblem you're looking for, and what model of Corvette you have. Do you happen to have your VIN available?*

Customer: **I want the chrome ones with the flags.**

Me: *... Alright. What model of Corvette is this for? That would make finding these a whole lot easier. Or should I just pick my favorite and go with that?*

Customer: **It's chrome and it's got the two flags... and it's got some red on the back.**

Me: *Okay. There are multiple Corvette emblems with crossed flags, could you please just tell me what kind of Corvette these are for.*

Customer: **Well, I got a Trailblazer SS and I'm gonna put them on my doors.**

Me: *You're going to put Corvette emblems on the doors of your... Okay. They're $55 a piece.*

Customer: **Why're they so expensive?**

Me: *I don't know, GM sets the prices.*

Customer: **Alright, I'm gonna come get some.**

[He bought five of them.]

[At the counter]

Customer: **Hey, how far back does your catalog go?**

Me: *Well, it depends on the car.*

Customer: **Does it go back to 1967?**

Me: *Only for Corvettes.*

Customer: **Alright man, cool. Well I got a '67 Impala and I need all of the brackets. I put a new engine in it and everything is on the wrong side.**

Me: *Okay, that's not a Corvette.*

Customer: **Sure it is, they're all the same.**

[Okay, it's not just trucks... according to my customers every car GM has ever made is the same.]

Me: *Hello, Parts.*

Customer: **Hi, I have an Impala. What's that part on the top?**

Me: *On top of what?*

Customer: **On top of my car! It looks like an antenna, but I don't think it's an antenna.**

Me: *It's an antenna.*

Customer: **Ohhhhh, is that what that is? I need one of those.**

[The urge to say 'government tracking device' was very high.]

[At the counter]

Me: *Hi, is there something I can help you with? [Silence] Hello? Hi, is there something I can help you with?*

Customer: **Need a license plate bracket for a Camaro.**

Me: *Alright, what year is your Camaro?*

Customer: **'14.**

Me: *I've got that in stock it's about $28, would you like me to grab one for you? [Silence] [More silence] Alright, I'll take silence as a yes. Let me get this for you. [Grabs the part and returns with it and the bill] Just take that to the cashier and she'll get you ready to go.*

Customer: **I'm not going to pay for that.**

Me: *Alright, I will gladly keep it. Have a lovely rest of your day.*

Customer: **How about this, you pay for this [Drops a citation on the counter] and then I'll pay for it. I'm not going to pay for anything.**

Me: *Okay, I didn't get you a ticket. I don't have the faintest idea who you even are.*

Customer: **Well, I got this ticket because of you, so how about I just give it to you, and I'll take my parts.**

Me: *Yeeeaaah... this really doesn't work that way, even a little. Sounds like you probably need to speak to your salesman.*

[I was always amazed at the things that were somehow specifically my fault.]

[At the counter]

Me: *Hi, is there something I can help you with?*

Customer: **What do they wash cars with?**

Me: *... uh... Soap?*

Customer: **No, out in the shop.**

Me: *Soap? ... I don't know, they have their own stuff out there.*

Customer: **But what do they wash the cars with?**

Me: *I don't know, they buy their own supplies for that stuff.*

Customer: **But what do they wash the cars with?**

Me: *I'm not sure I'm understanding you properly.*

Customer: **Sell me some of what they use.**

Me: *... Well... I can't really do that. I have GM stuff, if you'd like some of that?*

Customer: **You can't just go put some of their stuff in a jar and sell it to me?**

Me: *... ... Unfortunately, no... I can't do that.*

[Hmmmm, where can I get some car soap? I know! I won't go to a parts store, or any other retail store... I'll go to the dealership! But I won't buy the conveniently pre-packaged products; that would be idiotic! Instead, I'll pester the Parts Department for a mason jar of soap from their garage! BRILLIANT!]

Me: *Hello, Parts.*

Customer: **Yeah, I got a '02 Trailblazer, and I need that arm.**

Me: *... Which arm? There are lots of arms in a vehicle.*

Customer: **Well, I don't know. You're supposed to know. You're the parts guy.**

Me: *Indeed, I am. However, since I don't know who you are, and am not familiar with the individual issues of your vehicle, it's kinda difficult for me to make an accurate diagnosis over the phone.*

Customer: **... I don't know what you just said, but alright. I'll call you back.**

Me: *Hello, Parts.*

Customer: **I need... a... driver's passenger's door handle.**

Me: *Uhhh... What kind of car do you have?*

Customer: **It's a L...TZ...**

Me: *Well, LTZ is a trim package... What sort of vehicle is it?*

Customer: **It's a Suburban... 2... 005?**

Me: *And we're looking for the driver's door handle?*

Customer: **Driver's passenger's.**

Me: *Passenger's door handle? Is it on the driver's side or the passenger's side of the vehicle?*

Customer: **It's on the driver's side.**

Me: *So you need a driver's door handle?*

Customer: **No man, not the door that I sit in, the other one.**

Me: *I'm going to take a shot in the dark here, because I'm clearly not understanding properly... Are you looking for a rear door handle?*

Customer: **Yeah man, for the driver's passenger.**

[This makes so much more sense when it's written down.]

Me: *Hello, Parts.*

Customer: **Yeah, a rock hit my windshield and cracked it. How much is it to replace that piece?**

Me: *What kind of car do you have?*

Customer: **Cruze.**

Me: *Okay... and what year is your Cruze?*

Customer: **'13.**

Me: *Well, looks like the windshield is about $390. If you'd like, I can get you over to Service and they can get you an estimate on installation.*

Customer: **Can't you just replace the bit that's broken?**

Me: *... Like cut out the cracked part and replace it?*

Customer: **Yeah. I don't need the whole thing, just that bit that's cracked.**

Me: *I don't think glass works that way...*

[At the counter]

Me: *Hi, is there something I can help you with?*

Customer: **Hello young man, my name is Sparky, and this is my daughter. Introduce yourself.**

Daughter: **Well, my name is Summer, but I don't like that, so I go by Kiki.**

Me: *... It's a... uhh... pleasure to meet you both. Is there something I can help you with?*

Sparky: **Nah, we're just wandering.**

Me: *Okie doke. Well, if you need help with parts, you know where to find me.*

[These people looked exactly the way you're imagining.]

Me: *Hello, Parts.*

Customer: **Yeah, I need a stun anger.**

Me: *Did you just say "stun anger?"*

Customer: **Yeah, I need the stun anger.**

Me: *... ... Alright, what kind of vehicle is this for?*

Customer: **'02 van.**

Me: *And we're looking for the... stun anger...?*

Customer: **Yeah, how much does it cost?**

Me: *Roughly where in the car is the... stun anger located?*

Customer: **By the wheel.**

Me: *Are we looking for a steering angle sensor?*

Customer: **Yeah, I need one of them. How much does it cost?**

Me: *Hello, Parts.*

Customer: **Yeah, I was wondering how much that... pipe is.**

Me: *Alright, well, what kind of vehicle do you have?*

Customer: **I think it's... an '02.**

Me: *Okay, it's an '02... what?*

Customer: **It's... an '02... Chevy.**

Me: *...Alright, what variety of '02 Chevy is it?*

Customer: **It's... a truck.**

Me: *Okay... and is your '02 Chevy truck a 1500, 2500, or 3500 series?*

Customer: **Oh... uhhhhh... I don't know that.**

Me: *Would you happen to have your VIN available?*

Customer: **Well, I'm driving it right now. How much is that pipe at the back?**

Me: *Well, I'd love to help you, but we still don't even know what kind of truck you have... so it's going to be difficult to figure that out. If you could get that information and call me back, that would excellent.*

Customer: **Can't you just give me an idea what it costs?**

Me: *I don't know what pipe we're looking for, but I would estimate somewhere between $50 and $1000.*

Customer: **Oh... I'll call you back.**

[We often got calls from the customer service reps at GM]

CSR: **Hi, I have a customer on the phone and he needs to know how big the bushings are.**

Me: *... Okay, what sort of car and what bushings?*

CSR: **The front and the back bushings.**

Me: *The front and rear of what? And what sort of car is it?*

CSR: **The car is a [papers shuffling] 2001 Suburban, and he needs to know what size are the front and rear bushings.**

Me: *The front and rear of what? You need to give me more information to work with. There are a lot of bushings in a car.*

CSR: **Can you provide me with information on all of the bushing in the vehicle?**

Me: *No. Absolutely not. There are hundreds of bushings in a car. If you could just tell me what it's for, this would be really easy.*

CSR: **Ummm it's for the bumper?**

Me: *No, it's not.*

CSR: **It's for the stabilizer shaft?**

Me: *That sounds more likely.*

[Honestly, I would rather the customer just called us... which, if you're already this far, you know is saying quite a lot.]

Me: *Hello, Parts.*

Customer: **Yeah, what's that Chevy up by [local town]?**

Me: *That would be [local dealership].*

Customer: **Yeah... them. What're their hours today?**

Me: *I honestly don't know, they're an independently owned and operated franchise.*

Customer: **Well you work for Chevy, right?**

Me: *I do, indeed.*

Customer: **Then you should know.**

Me: *Unfortunately, as I just said, they are a different business, and I don't know. I'll gladly give you their number and you could call them and find out.*

Customer: **Nah man, whatever. [Hangs up]**

[411 is on backorder. I can get you those hours in about 4 - 6 weeks.]

Me: *Hello, Parts.*

Customer: **I got a... I got a... I got a... ... ...**

Me: *... ... You have a?*

Customer: **I got a... '89 Caprice. I need you all to sell me some tools.**

Me: *Tools, as in to fix a car?*

Customer: **Yeah, I need a whole bunch.**

Me: *Okay, unfortunately, we don't sell tools.*

Customer: **Well how am I supposed to fix my car?**

Me: *If you'd like, we have a garage full of techs, I could get you in touch with Service and they could check it out.*

Customer: **Could I just bring it there and use your tools?**

Me: *No.*

Customer: **Well why not?**

Me: *... Because... just... no. I'm sorry, we don't do that.*

Customer: **Oh, alright. [Hangs up]**

Me: *Hello, Parts.*

Customer: **Yeah, see, it's got this metal pipe that runs along the top of it, and there's a metal part and a rubber part, and I need that seal at the metal end.**

Me: *Whoa, whoa, whoa. Okay, let's take a few steps back and start at the beginning. What kind of car is this for?*

Customer: **Man, it's not for a car, it's for a fork lift.**

Me: *Sir, this is a General Motors dealer ship, I can't help you.*

[And yet, still not as out there as the person who insisted they bought parts for their dishwasher from me.]

Me: *Hello, Parts.*

Customer: **Yeah man, I got a '05, and I need that dome lamp.**

Me: *Okie doke, and what kind of '05 vehicle do you have?*

Customer: **It's a '05... uh... Pontiac Bonneville.**

Me: *Alright, and we're looking for the dome lamp?*

Customer: **Yeah man, the dome lamp on the passenger's side.**

Me: *Passenger's side? According to my catalog, this vehicle only has one dome lamp...*

Customer: **What are you talking about? Every car has two!**

Me: *Okay... Is this 'dome lamp' on the interior or the exterior of the vehicle?*

Customer: **Man, it's on the exterior.**

Me: *Front or rear?*

Customer: **They in the front, just like every car.**

Me: *So we're looking for a headlamp?*

Customer: **Well yeah, if that's what you want to call it.**

[It's not 'what I want to call it'... it's what the part has actually been called... for over 100 years...]

[Seriously?]

"Yeah, I just got a car and it's got some little punk-ass horn in it. I need a manly horn, something that'll scare the shit outta some folks."

"I like coming home to my wife at the end of the day and seeing she hasn't been murdered."

"Thank you very much, you've been a big help. I'm gonna call up and get you some stickers, and maybe a Coke."

"Well that's great, but I won't trust anything a man says."

[Chapter 3]

You Got That In Stock?

Me:	*Hello, Parts.*
Customer:	**Hi, I just put a new radio in my '04 Malibu, and now my blinker lights come on by themselves, so I need that cable that connects the radio to the blinkers at the front. I think it's in the steering column.**
Me:	*... A cable that connects your... radio directly to your front lights? And it's in the steering column?*
Customer:	**Yeah, that's the one, it's in the column.**
Me:	*That's... not a thing. There's no cable that connects your radio to your headlights.*
Customer:	**Sure there is! Why else would I be having this problem?**
Me:	*Okay... Unfortunately, I'm not familiar with anything like that being in any of our vehicles... If you could bring this cable in, maybe that would help me find it for you?*
Customer:	**Well... I haven't actually looked at it yet, so I don't know what all is in there, but I'll bring you something.**

[Needless to say, he never showed up.]

Me: *Hello, Parts.*

Customer: **Yeah, I've got a Dodge Grand, and I need those clips by the trans. You have those? I called the Parts Department.**

Me: *Um... Yes, this is the Parts Department. What kind of vehicle did you have? We don't have parts for Dodges...*

Customer: **It's a Dodge... Grand Prix... '07.**

Me: *It's a Pontiac?*

Customer: **Well I thought it was a Dodge.**

Me: *Okay... and you're looking for what?*

Customer: **Those bits back by the transmission.**

Me: *...The fittings for the cooler lines?*

Customer: **Yeah, I want some of those.**

Me: *I've got those in stock, they're about $20 for the pair.*

Customer: **Alright, I want them, and cancel those Dodge pads I ordered earlier. I called the Parts Department. [Hangs up]**

[I thought it was a Dodge... so I called a Chevy dealership.]

Me: *Hello, Parts.*

Customer: **I need tires. How much they cost?**

Me: *... Okay, what size tires are you looking for?*

Customer: **I got a truck.**

Me: *Alright, but what size tires are you looking for?*

Customer: **My truck's got 16" wheels.**

Me: *Okay, but what size tires are you looking for?*

Customer: **What comes on those new trucks?**

Me: *They have Bridgestones, Firestones, Goodyears, or Generals.*

Customer: **Okay, well that's what I want.**

Me: *Alright, but what size tires are you looking for?*

Customer: **I want those ones for my truck.**

Me: *We've established that, but unless you tell me the complete size of the tire, I'm not going to be able to help you. There are three sets of numbers on the tire, like 225 / 50 / 18, if you get me those numbers I can help you.*

Customer: **Well those numbers you just said sound right, how much are those?**

Me: *Those numbers are 18" car tires, they're not going to fit on your wheels.*

Customer: **Oh, well that ain't what I want then. How much are Goodyears?**

Me: *You still haven't told me what size tires you're looking for.*

Customer: **Oh, I need to know what size they are? I'm gonna have to call you back.**

[If only that had been the first question I had asked... or the second... or third... or fourth...]

Me: *Hello, Parts.*

Customer: **You got a light for a dump truck?**

Me: *You're going to have to be a bit more specific than that.*

Customer: **I'll say it slower. You. Got. A. Light. For. A. Dump. Truck?**

Me: *No.*

Customer: **You ain't even look.**

Me: *No, I'm just that good.*

Customer: **Man, fuck you. [Hangs up]**

[I'm going to become rich and famous one day when I invent a device that lets you punch people in the face over the phone.]

Me: *Hello, Parts.*

Customer: **DO I DRIVE IN THE D OR IN THE D WITH THE CIRCLE AROUND IT?!**

Me: *Uh.... say what now?*

Customer: **FORGET IT! SEND ME TO SERVICE! THEY'LL TELL ME!**

Me: *Absolutely, hang on one second.*

[I feel like we really connected.]

Me: *Hello, Parts.*

Customer: **Yeah, do you all have a blower motor resistor for a 2004 Grand Prix?**

Me: *I certainly should, let me have a look.*

Customer: **Hey, you ever hear of a precipitator?**

Me: *Uhh... no.*

Customer: **Oh, well they tell me I need a precipitator. What about a aviator window? You heard of one of those? I need one of them too.**

Me: *Uhhh... I'm pretty confident that's not a thing.*

Customer: **They said it's by the blower.**

Me: *No... there are definitely no precipitators or aviator windows by your blower.*

Customer: **Well why'd they tell me I need 'em then?**

[Man, if I could answer that question, I sure as hell wouldn't be working here.]

Me: *Hello, Parts.*

Customer: **Yeah man, I need them wafers.**

Me: *I think you might have called the wrong number.*

Customer: **Is this Parts?**

Me: *Yup.*

Customer: **Yeah, like I said, I need them wafers up in the lock.**

Me: *I have no idea what we're talking about. Cars don't have wafers in them.*

Customer: **They're up in that lock by the steering wheel.**

Me: *I'm sorry, I really don't know about any wafers in the locks. You might be better off talking to a locksmith.*

Customer: **Man, I am a locksmith. You all don't sell them wafers separate?**

[If I'm honest, this one was a bit on me, because "wafers" ended up being a more common slang for lock cylinder tumblers than I anticipated.]

Me: *Hello, Parts.*

Customer: **Yeah, I need a transfer case gasket for a '96 Chevy. You got one of those?**

Me: *Okay, we're going to have to be a bit more specific than that... what kind of '96 Chevy?*

Customer: **Tahoe.**

Me: *Alright, what engine does it have?*

Voice in the Background: *The hell does he need to know what engine it has?! Why they asking you shit like that?*

Customer: **[Yelling] Bitch, shut the fuck up! I'm trying to use the phone! He doesn't give a shit what you think anyhow! [Calm] It has a 5.7 in it.**

Me: *Ooookay... thank you... yes, I have one of those gaskets in stock... it's $10.*

Customer: **I'll be there in a minute.**

[uhhhhhhhhhhh...]

Me: *Hello, Parts.*

Customer: **I got one'a them Camaros and I need that wire.**

Me: *Okay, what year is your Camaro, and which wire are we talking about?*

Customer: **It's a SS, and I need that wire up in the front.**

Me: *Okay... what year is your SS Camaro, and which wire are we talking about?*

Customer: **It's that wire up in the front. I ran into something and bent all the wires.**

Me: *Alright, well... I still need to know what year it is and which wire we're talking about.*

Customer: **Man, it's the wires up in the front! I keep telling you that.**

Me: *I understand that, but there are a lot of wires in the front of a car.*

Customer: **Well, I need the ones I broke.**

Me: *Alright, well, without some more information, I'm not going to be able to help you.*

Customer: **Man, whatever. [Hangs up]**

[I should have kept a Ouija board to help with people like this.]

[First call of Saturday morning]

Me: *Hello, Parts.*

Customer: **You all open right now?**

Me: *If I wasn't open, I wouldn't have answered the phone.*

Customer: **Man, you all need to be stopped.**

Me: *I have no idea what that means.*

Customer: **Man, fuck you. [Hangs up]**

[The first customer of Saturday morning was always something special.]

Me: *Hello, Parts.*

Customer: **You got Chrysler tires?**

Me: *... Maybe, what size tire you looking for?*

Customer: **Chrysler.**

Me: *No no no, what size tire, like 15", 16", 17", something like that... There'll be 3 sets of numbers on your tires like 215 / 60 / 16.*

Customer: **200.**

Me: *No, that's not a tire size. What do the numbers on the tires say?*

Customer: **It says C-h-r-y...**

Me: *No, those aren't numbers. I need the three sets of numbers off the tire.*

Customer: **They ain't just Chrysler tires?**

Me: *No.*

Customer: **I'm gonna have to call you back.**

Me: *Hello, Parts.*

Customer: **Hi, I need a new key for my 2006, Oldsmobile Savannah.**

Me: *... Um... I'm sorry, Oldsmobile never made a car called the Savannah, and the company was defunct in 2004... Are you sure that's what kind of car you have?*

Customer: **Of course I'm sure what kind of car I have! It's a 2006, Oldsmobile Savannah!**

Me: *Alright... Well, my catalog has no listing for that make and model. If you could just go to the car and tell me what it says on the back, that would be really helpful.*

Customer: **[Walks to car] It says Pontiac Montana.**

[Of course I'm sure what kind of car I have...Also, it was a 2009...This conversation is why this book exists. At the time, it was the single stupidest moment I had experienced at the counter... Oh, to be so young and naive again.]

Me: *Hello, Parts.*

Customer: **Yeah, I need the Parts Department!**

Me: *This is the Parts Department, how can I help you?*

Customer: **I need to get the Parts Department!**

Me: *Uh... okay, one second, let me transfer you...*
             [Put call on hold. Pick back up]
             Hello, Parts.

Customer: **Yeah, Parts Department? I need the gribadurstraka for my car. You got one'a them?**

Me: *You need the... gri...ba..durstraka?*

Customer: **Yeah, I need one'a them for my car.**

Me: *Uh, okay, I'm a little unclear what we're looking for.*

Customer: **You know, it's that little piece that holds the door closed.**

Me: *So we need a... glove box... door striker?*

Customer: **You got one? I'mma come up there and get one. [Hangs up]**

[I apologize if I spelled gribadurstraka wrong.]

[At the counter]

Me: *Hi, is there something I can help you with?*

Customer: **I need the oil... ... ... and the filter.**

Me: *...Alright. for what sort of car?*

Customer: **Uhhh... I don't know... it's outside.**

Me: *Is it your car?*

Customer: **Yeah, it's mine.**

Me: *And you don't know what kind of car you own?*

Customer: **Uhhhh... no... let me go look.**

[He never came back, so I assume it wasn't a Chevrolet.]

Me: *Hello, Parts.*

Customer: **Yeah man, my transmission is poppin'.**

Me: *Well, th-that's a good thing... right?*

Customer: **No it ain't!**

Me: *Oh, my apologies, I guess I'm unfamiliar with the terminology.*

Customer: **I need to know if that's covered up under my power steering.**

Me: *Covered under... your power steering? Like... physically?*

Customer: **Man, you don't know what you're talking about. [Hangs up]**

[I rarely know what I'm talking about.]

[Midway through a call]

Me: *I can hold these at the counter for you. Is there a name that I can put on them?*

Customer: **I've never dealt with you before.**

Me: *Okay... Well, I'm glad you called us, but could I get a name to hold these under?*

Customer: **I've never dealt with you before.**

Me: *Alright... I'll hold them at the counter under, "I've never dealt with you before."*

[After looking up a bunch of parts]

Customer:	**Can you fax that quote to me?**
Me:	*Sure, what's your fax number?*
Customer:	**Norman Hensley.**
Me:	*... Okay, and what is your fax number?*
Customer:	**Just send it to Norman Hensley.**
Me:	*So... I should just punch that into my fax machine and hit go?*
Customer:	**Yeah, that'll go to me.**
Me:	*Okay, I don't think you understand how fax machines work. I need a phone number with another fax machine attached to it.*
Customer:	**Oh... uh... well I don't have one of those.**
Me:	*... Alright, then how am I supposed to fax this to you?*
Customer:	**Uh... uh... I'll call you back. [Hangs up]**

[I like to imagine this guy sitting next to his toaster, eagerly waiting for this message to pop up.]

Me: *Hello, Parts.*

Customer: **Yeah, my car keys are stuck in the wall, and I need you to make me a new one.**

Me: *Your keys are... stuck in a wall?*

Customer: **Yeah, behind my mailbox.**

Me: *Alright... Well, in order to make you a new key, I'm going to need the title or original bill of sale, a valid registration, and a valid driver's license, all with matching names and addresses.*

Customer: **I need all that, just because my keys are stuck in the wall?**

Me: *...Uh ...Yes.*

Customer: **But I don't have any of that!**

Me: *I'm sorry, there are no exceptions. Perhaps a locksmith might be a better option.*

Customer: **Will he be able to get my keys out of the wall?**

Me: *Yeah, absolutely; locksmiths are great at stuff like that.*

Customer: **Alright, I'm going to go call him then.**

Me: *Hello, Parts.*

Customer: **Where... I want... ... where is that... area?**

Me: *P-pardon me?*

Customer: **I want... that... area.**

Me: *I'm kinda lost... is there a parts problem I can help you with?*

Customer: **I want that... that area where they fix the cars.**

Me: *The Service Department? One second, let me transfer you.*

Me: *Hello, Parts.*

Customer: **Yes, I have a '12 Buick Lacrosse, and I need the axis.**

Me: *You need an... axle?*

Customer: **No, it says here I need multiple axis.**

Me: *I'm not entirely sure what I'm looking for... Do you know where it is in the car?*

Customer: **No, I don't know where it is.**

Me: *Alright, do we know what system it's in? Perhaps the suspension or brakes?*

Customer: **No, I don't know that.**

Me: *Okay... do we know what it does or controls?*

Customer: **No, I don't know that either. Do you have one there?**

Me: *Well, we still don't know what you're even looking for... so there's no way for me to know if I have stock it.*

Customer: **How about any other dealers, do they have one?**

Me: *Probably. There's bound to be at least one dealership that stocks it...*

Customer: **Alright, well, I'm going to call them then.**
[Hangs up]

Me: *Hello, Parts.*

Customer: **MY CAR WON'T START!**

Me: *Okay... well, how can I help you?*

Customer: **IT'S YOUR FAULT AND YOU GOTTA COME FIX IT!**

Me: *My fault? That doesn't really sound like something I would do.*

Customer: **YOU FIXED MY CAR AND NOW IT WON'T START, AND YOU ALL NEED TO TAKE RESPONSIBILITY FOR WHAT YOU DID.**

Me: *Ma'am, this is the Parts Department, all I do is look up parts... at no point have I ever so much as feigned fixing a customer's car.*

Customer: **Oh... uh... WELL WHO AM I SUPPOSED TO YELL AT THEN?!**

Me: *Let me get you in touch with Service, hopefully they'll have some answers for you.*

Customer: **FORGET IT [Hangs up]**

[These people always got sent to the Service Writer who had bothered me the most that day.]

Me: *Hello, Parts.*

Customer: **Yes, I need a price on... hang on a second...
            [To someone off the phone] Anthony.
            Anthony! Anthony. Anthony. Anthony!**

Me: *Uhh... hello?*

Customer: **[Still off the phone] Anthony. Anthony!
            Anthony. Anthony! Anthony. Anthony.**

Me: *Hello? Is everything okay? I'm going to hang up
            if you're not going to talk to me.*

Customer: **[To me] Hang on one second.
            [Off the phone] Anthony. Anthony. Anthony.
            Anthony! Anthony.**

Me: *Okay, yeah, I'm going to go now. Feel free to try
            again when you have some more free time.*

Customer: **[Still off phone] Anthony. Anthony! Anthony.**

Me: *[Hangs up]*

[I probably cut out half of the Anthonys.]

Me: *Hello, Parts.*

Customer: **Yeah, my car is in your shop, and I wanted to know if my part came in.**

Me: *Yes it did. It came in this morning, and it's out in the shop already.*

Customer: **Now, they ain't gonna make me put it on myself, are they?**

Me: *You brought it in to us for service, right?*

Customer: **Yeah, I brought it to you all for the service.**

Me: *Okay, then one of our techs will be putting it on your car for you.*

Customer: **Oh... well that's good, because I wouldn't know where it goes.**

[He sounded genuinely concerned.]

[Chapter 4]

Is That With My Discount?

Me: *Hello, Parts.*

Customer: **WHERE ARE YOU?!**

Me: *Uh... I'm at my desk? Is there something I can help you with?*

Customer: **I'm standing at your counter, and I need some service!**

Me: *[Walks to the counter]*

Sir, I'm now standing at my counter, and there's definitely no one here.

Customer: **Nuh uh! I'm right here at the Parts Department.**

Me: *At what dealership?*

Customer: **... Oh... Wait a minute. [Hangs up]**

[Sometimes I wonder how these people manage to dress themselves.]

Me: *Hello, Parts.*

Customer: **You have a Nissan Maxima?**

Me: *No, I have a Chevy Sonic. Is there something I can help you with?*

Customer: **You don't have a Nissan Maxima?**

Me: *No. I don't. Is there a car part issue that I can help you with?*

Customer: **I want a Nissan Maxima.**

Me: *Okay, let me get you to the operator. She'll get you someone in Sales.*

[The phrase you were looking for was, "Sorry, I wanted to speak to Sales. I would like to purchase a Nissan Maxima." Sometimes words are difficult.]

Me: *Hello, Parts.*

Customer: **I have a 1999 Corvette, and I need a battery for it.**

Me: *Alright, that should just be a standard 78 - series battery. I have those in stock. You'd be looking at $139 plus tax.*

Customer: **Standard?! You don't put standard parts in a Corvette! You put professional parts in a Corvette! I need you to get me a professional battery!**

Me: *... Well, looks like you're in luck, I have a... professional battery... on sale, today only, for $139 plus tax.*

Customer: **You do? I'll be there to get it in just a minute.**

[Corvette owners...]

Me: *Hello, Parts.*

Customer: **Yeah, I need a clutch.**

Me: *Alright, for what kind of car?*

Customer: **It's for my car.**

Me: *Okay, and what sort of car do you have?*

Customer: **Why you askin' me that? I'm gonna call a different dealership. [Hangs up]**

[Yes...What complete madness it is that I might need to know what car you own in order to get you parts... I'll just guess in the future.]

Me: *Hello, Parts.*

Customer: **800 dash 41.**

Me: *Uh, okay, and what exactly is that?*

Customer: **It's a part number. I don't know what it's called, but I need one.**

Me: *Alright, well that's not a GM part number.*

Customer: **How about 800 dash 42?**

Me: *Okay, that's not a GM part number either.*

Customer: **How do you know?**

Me: *I know, because I've spent 50 hours a week, for years of my life, looking up parts.*

Customer: **Man, I'm just gonna call someone who knows what they're talking about.**

[I knew they were aftermarket heater hose connectors...]

[At the counter]

Me: Hi, is there something I can help you with?

Customer: ... ... **Module.**

Me: Okay. How about we start with a make and model of the vehicle?

Customer: ... ...

Me: Should I just guess?

Customer: ... . **Grand Prix.**

Me: Alright, what year is the car and what module are you looking for?

Customer: ... ... **Why you askin' me all these questions? I just need the module.**

Me: Sir, there are a lot of modules in a car, I only ask questions so I can get you the correct parts.

Customer: ... ... **They ain't ask me all these questions at Auto Zone. I'm just gonna go back there.**

Me: I wish you all the best of luck.

[Oh wait! Stupid me. I forgot there's only a single module across every vehicle of the 8 different makes that GM operates. My bad.]

Me: *Hello, Parts.*

Customer: **I got a '09, and what do you call that connector?**

Me: *... ... ... What?*

Customer: **It's a '09, and I need to know what that connector is called.**

Me: *... ... ... Do you have your VIN available?*

Customer: **You need a VIN to tell me what that connector is called?**

Me: *... It's probably just called a connector?*

Customer: **Well I know it's called a connector, but I want to know what the connector is called.**

Me: *... W... w-what? I'm going to need a VIN.*

Customer: **[Long sigh] ... [Hangs up]**

[Sometimes you insist on getting a VIN just because you know it'll end the call...]

[Midway through a conversation]

Me: *Could I get the last 8 digits of your VIN?*

Customer: **But that's on the car outside, and I'm in the house.**

Me: *I understand that, but I still need those numbers.*

Customer: **You want the last 3?**

Me: *Eight, the last eight digits.*

Customer: **The first eight?**

Me: *The. Last. Eight. Digits.*

Customer: **So you want me to get the last 6 digits?**

Me: *Eight. I need Eight. Eight digits. Actually, just get the whole thing and call me back.*

[I never knew if people were messing with me, or if 8 was just a more difficult concept than I remembered... from when I was like... 3.]

Me: *Hello, Parts.*

Customer: **Yeah, man, I got a Saturn.**

Me: *That's... unfortunate... but we need to get a little more specific here. What kind of Saturn do you have?*

Customer: **Ahhh, man, I don't know. Whatever it is, it's a piece of shit.**

Me: *Okay, that may very well be, but I can't really look that up in my catalog.*

Customer: **Ahhhh, man, I think it's a Vue? What's it gonna cost me to get a transmission for this ffffucking piece of shit?**

Me: *Is it two wheel drive or all wheel drive?*

Customer: **Man, I don't give a shit. Which one is more expensive?**

Me: *Well, the all wheel drive one is about $3400.*

Customer: **$3400?! Man, I ain't never gonna get these mooks to pay no $3400 for no transmission. You know what, fuck it, I'm just gonna tell 'em they need a new car.**

[Pro tip: don't take your car to this shop.]

Me: *Hello, Parts.*

Customer: **Yeah, do you carry diesel clips?**

Me: *Diesel clips?*

Customer: **You know, those clips for the diesel.**

Me: *I'm sorry, I've never heard of a diesel clip.*

Customer: **Ugh, fine. I'll get 'em somewhere else.**

[Yeah, god forbid you waste a breath trying to clarify...]

Me:	*Hello, Parts.*
Customer:	**I have a Sierra, how much is a bolt for the oil pan?**
Me:	*Well, what year is your Sierra?*
Customer:	**1996. Do you have that bolt? How much is it?**
Me:	*Alright, I still need more information. Is it a 1500, 2500, or a 3500?*
Customer:	**I don't know what that means. Do you have that bolt?**
Me:	*Again, I need more information before I can even look up this bolt. Do you have the VIN number available?*
Customer:	**I don't know what that is. Do you have that bolt in stock? Can I come pick one up?**

[Oh oh oh. THAT bolt. Yes. I'm sorry. We just restocked the THAT bolt bin.]

Me: *Hello, Parts.*

Customer: **I need the intake tool.**

Me: *The intake tool?*

Customer: **Yeah, I need that tool that puts the air into my engine.**

Me: *Well, we don't sell tools.*

Customer: **Then how am I supposed to get the air into my engine?**

[That's one of the great mysteries of the universe.]

[The interior of the building was being remodeled]

Customer: **Excuse me! Excuse me! I need some assistance!**

Me: *Ma'am there's caution tape over that counter for a reason. Please follow the signs around to the Service entrance for Parts.*

Customer: **Nuh uh, I don't need to walk all the way over there! You gotta help me here!**

[Would it surprise you if I told you this was a Saturday?]

Me: *Hello, Parts.*

Customer: **Yes, I was wondering, if I gave you a VIN number, if you could tell me if this car's got a roof.**

Me: *Well, I sure hope it does... or it's going to be full of snow.*

[I don't know much about cars... but I thought this was a standard feature.]

[At the counter]

Me: *Hi, is there something I can help you with?*

Customer: **A couple hours ago, I saw a STS at the car wash, and I wanna know how much that is.**

Me: *Okay... this is the Parts Department, you're going to need to speak to Sales.*

Customer: **Well where am I supposed to go?**

Me: *To the... Sales Department?*

Customer: **Well where's that? You all ain't gonna direct me?**

Me: *It's right there [points] where all of the cars and salesmen are.*

Customer: **Well how do I get there?**

Me: *You... walk? It's literally 20 feet away.*

[It's like 80% of the interior of the building...]

[At the counter]

Me: *Hi, is there something I can help you with?*

Customer: **I need a refund.**

Me: *Okay, was there something wrong with the parts?*

Customer: **No, you just ordered them for the wrong truck.**

Me: *So, yesterday, when I asked you for your VIN, at least 5 times, and you refused to give it to me... You said "I'm not going to give you my VIN number," that's... my fault?*

Customer: **Yeah, you all ordered parts for the wrong truck, so I went somewhere else and got 'em.**

Me: *Alright, and how do you know the other parts are correct?*

Customer: **Well, I gave the other dealership my VIN number and they said the ones you all gave me were wrong.**

Me: *Yeah, you're right, that's very clearly my fault.*

Me: *Hello, Parts.*

Customer: **Alright, I need you to listen to me now. I got a '08 and I need the whole harness.**

Me: *Okay, what kind of '08, and what harness are we looking for?*

Customer: **I just told you to listen, and you ain't listened at all. It's a '08, and I need the whole harness. I ain't getting no fire up in the front, and I already replaced the harness four times.**

Me: *You... aren't getting any... fire? Well that sounds like a good thing; your car isn't supposed to be on fire.*

Customer: **Boy, you ain't listenin' at all are you? I ain't gettin' the fire up in the front, and I need to know how much that harness costs.**

Me: *... Could I get the last 8 digits of your VIN?*

Customer: **You ain't listenin', and now you gonna make me walk all the way out to the car? You know what, I'll call someone else.**

Me: *Okie doke, have a lovely day.*

[Out in the lot, looking at a customer's car]

Customer: **Hey, could I ask you a question right quick?**

Me: *Yeah man, what's up?*

Customer: **Is your name really Hollywood?**

Me: *Yup, I have really weird parents.*

Customer: **[Incredulous stare]**
I can't tell if you're for real right now.

Me: *No man, no joke, Hollywood Wellington.*
[Shakes hand]
Pleasure to meet you.

Customer: **[Even more incredulous stare]**

Me: *Alright, you caught me, my real name is Josh...*
this is just my nickname around here.

Customer: **Awww man, and here I was thinking I just**
got to meet a guy named Hollywood! You
should change your name.

[Hollywood was the name on my name tag... don't ask. This knowledge will be useful again later.]

Me: *Hello, Parts.*

Customer: **Let me tell you what happened. I was at the car wash and they busted them wings off the front of my car. How much do those cost?**

Me: *... Wings? I'm not super familiar with cars, but I'm pretty sure they don't have wings.*

Customer: **Well they busted them off, and I need to know how much they cost.**

Me: *Okay... What kind of car do you have? And I'm still not sure what 'wings' we're talking about.*

Customer: **It's a Equinox, and they're those wings right up in the middle in the front.**

Me: *Are you looking for... a grille emblem?*

Customer: **Yeah, them wings up on the front.**

[After getting 99% through looking something up]

Me: *Could I get your VIN, there are a few weird options on these.*

Customer: **[Aggressive sigh] Ugh, I'm trying to put gas in my car right now.**

Me: *My apologies, I didn't mean to inconvenience you... You called me after all.*

[If you're putting gas in your car, that means you're standing RIGHT THERE! This is literally the most convenient time for you to be asked this question!]

Me: *Hello, Parts.*

Customer: **Yeah man, I got a '02 Trailblazer, and I need a new MC.**

Me: *Have you tried Jay-Z? He's usually a pretty solid bet.*

Customer: **What? No man, I need a new MC for my car.**

Me: *Are we maybe talking about a PCM? Are you looking for the car's computer?*

Customer: **No, I don't need that; I need a new MC.**

Me: *Alright... I just don't know what that is, so I'm going to stick with Jay-Z.*

[5 minutes later, we figured out that he needed... a PCM... what a surprise.]

Me: *Hello, Parts.*

Customer: **Are you Victor?**

Me: *I am not. Victor is in Sales. This is the Parts Department. I can get you to the operator and she can get you to him.*

Customer: **So you're telling me you aren't Victor?**

Me: *Correct. Victor is in Sales. Let me get you to the operator and she can get him for you.*

Customer: **...Well, why aren't you Victor?**

Me: *Let me get you to the operator.*

[It's not often that my customers got so existential. Why am I not Victor?]

Me: *Hello, Parts.*

Customer: **Yeah, you all can fix my car.**

Me: *Uh... pardon me?*

Customer: **You called and asked if you could fix my car.**

Me: *... No, you called me.*

Customer: **Oh. [Hangs up]**

[Realistically, this person got bounced to Parts on accident, and I just didn't realize...]

[At the counter]

Me: *Hi, is there something I can help you with?*

Customer: **[Blank stare]**

Me: *Hello? Hi, this is the Parts Department, is there anything I can help you with?*

Customer: **... ... ... Shooter.**

Me: *Pardon me?*

Customer: **... ... ... Shooter... for a Monte Carlo.**

Me: *Okay, what year Monte Carlo? And are we maybe talking about a washer fluid nozzle?*

Customer: **... ... '02...**

               [Takes three steps back and continues staring at me.]

Me: *I'm going to assume that's a yes on the nozzle thing. Those are about $24 plus tax. I'd have to order them.*

Customer: **[Blank stare] Why so much?**

Me: *I'm sorry, I don't set the prices. Would you like me to order these for you?*

Customer: **... I need... two... [Walks away]**

[Questions I've Been Asked...]

"I don't know what kind of car it is, but it's reeeeeeal old and I need a oil pan for it. You all got one of them?"

"I think my car is leaking something... could you look at my nipples?"

"Ummm, yes, is it bad for your paint if a bird dookies on your car?"

"Hi. How you doin' today? I need that bolt, that bolt up in the middle. How you doin' today? That bolt up in the hood, between the middle and that thing that comes up. I got a Suburban. How you doin'? That bolt up in the middle by that part that comes up. You got one of those?"

[Chapter 5]

I Lost My Keys

[A phrase that still gives me nightmares.]

[At the counter]

Me: *Hi, is there som...*

Customer: **Need a key. [Drops keys on counter]**

Me: *Okay, what kind of car do you...*

Customer: **My VIN is in your system!**

Me: *Alright, can I get your name, so I can look it up?*

Customer: **I just said, my VIN is your system!**

Me: *Yes... I got that... but it's just that I can't pull it up without at least knowing your name.*

Customer: **[Shaking keys] You know what, forget it, just make me a key! [Hits keys on the counter]**

Me: *Sorry, I just remembered my key machine is broken.*

Customer: **That's what you fuckers told me last time!**

Me: *Well, it's still broken. Hopefully it'll be fixed on Monday.*

Customer: **What time do you open on Monday?! Because I'm coming back and it better be fucking working! [Walks away]**

[It was weird how often that machine stopped working when people started acting like assholes... I'm sure it was just a coincidence.]

[Midway through a call]

Me: *No, unfortunately we don't have that, and the part is discontinued through General Motors. There's no longer stock available.*

Customer: **So do you have one there?**

Me: *No. The part is discontinued. There's no stock available in the whole country.*

Customer: **So does [dealership up the road] have one?**

[Discontinued: Adjective. Permanently no longer available or in production.]

Me:	*Hello, Parts.*
Customer:	**Why did you put me on hold?!**
Me:	*Pardon me? I haven't put anyone hold... I literally just picked up the phone.*
Customer:	**Well, I need to know how much it's going to be to fix my car!**
Me:	*Okay, this is Parts, it sounds like you need to speak to Service. I can transfer you out there.*
Customer:	**Oh my god, you don't know?! [Aggressive sigh] Just tell me what it costs!**
Me:	*Okay, let me transfer you to Service; they'll get you all the information you need.*
Customer:	**No!**
Me:	*Excuse me?*
Customer:	**No! Don't you dare transfer me! You get the information and you tell me! Right now!**
Me:	*Let me get you to the Service Department, they will be able to assist you.*
Customer:	**[Hangs up]**

[Open the counter Saturday Morning... there's a guy staring at me.]

Customer: **I need a part.**

Me: *... ..... Alright, what sort of part?*

Customer: **I ordered it.**

Me: *Okay, what name was it ordered under?*

              [Gets his name... There's nothing ordered.]

              Well, it doesn't look like I have anything here.

Customer: **I ordered it a while ago.**

Me: *How long ago is "a while?"*

Customer: **Ohhhhh, I think maybe a year or two. You don't have it anymore? I need to get it.**

Me: *You ordered it potentially two years ago, and you're just coming to get it now? No. We don't have it anymore. Do you have your VIN, we need to start from scratch.*

Customer: **No, I don't have that. [Walks away]**

Me:	*Hello, Parts.*
Customer:	**I was just talking to someone and they said you would make me a key.**
Me:	*Okay, I'm going to need proof of ownership of the vehicle...*
Customer:	**Well... you see, this is a special circumstance, and you need to accommodate me.**
Me:	*I'm sorry, there are no special circumstances. No exceptions.*
Customer:	**Alright, now listen to me, you need to make an exception. You need to accommodate me!**
Me:	*Nope. I'd be happy to assist you, but you're going to need to supply me with proof of ownership of the vehicle.*
Customer:	**But I don't have that!**
Me:	*I can't make you a key for a car without proof that you own it.*
Customer:	**Well that's a stupid rule.**

[Is it though? We had people on the reg who were clearly trying to get keys for cars they didn't own... see page 131.]

Me:	*Hello, Parts.*
Customer:	**I need a cover for an Impala.**
Me:	*Alright, what kind of cover and what year Impala?*
Customer:	**It's a '02.**
Me:	*Okay, and what kind of cover are we looking for.*
Customer:	**That one up on the engine.**
Me:	*Okay, the front cover is $299. We would have to order it.*
Customer:	**What's the shop price?**
Me:	*Are you with a shop?*
Customer:	**No.**
Me:	*Then the shop price shouldn't concern you.*
Customer:	**Fine, I'll set one up then, now you gonna tell me what it is?**
Me:	*It's $280, how does that sound?*
Customer:	**Man, you a fuckin' asshole.**
Me:	*Buh bye. [Hangs up]*

[I'm not with a shop, but I will establish a whole damn business just to get a discount on this single part...]

Me: *Hello, Parts.*

Customer: **It's a '08 Silverado... No a 0'10 Silverado.**

Me: *...Alright... Well, what're you looking for?*

Customer: **It's a '08 Silverado.**

Me: *Indeed, it is. What sort of parts are we looking for?*

Customer: **Oh... Well, it's for a '08 Silverado.**

Me: *Of course. It's an '08 Silverado, and we need a part for it?*

Customer: **Yeah...**

Me: *And what part are we looking for?*

Customer: **A... uh... A Silverado.**

Me: *...Alright... that's... that's not a part...*

Customer: **Well... that's what I need...**

[Do I send him to Sales?]

Me: *Hello, Parts.*

Customer: **Hi, I'm up here from Florida, and I'm stuck at a hotel and my keys are locked in my truck, so I need you to make me a new one from my VIN number.**

Me: *Well, before I can do that I'm going to need you to supply me with three things: the title or original bill of sale; a valid registration; and a valid driver's license; all documents need to have the same names and addresses across them.*

Customer: **Everyone keeps telling me that same shit. I have all of that, but it's in my glove box, and I can't get it.**

Me: *Well, unfortunately, due to rules imposed on us by the Secretary of State, I'm required to have all of those documents before I can cut a key from a VIN.*

Customer: **Well that's stupid! Everyone keeps that shit in their glove box!**

Me: *You really shouldn't keep the title of your vehicle inside your car, if someone were to break in and sign that, they become the legal owner of that vehicle.*

Customer: **You know what, fuck you. [Hangs up]**

[Just trying to help... ish.]

Me: *Hello, Parts.*

Customer: **I need a harmonica for a '71 box truck.**

Me: *Nope.*

Customer: **So you don't have one?**

Me: *I do not.*

Customer: **Man, no one has this thing. [Hangs up]**

[Guarantee it was a harmonic balancer, but I wasn't about to touch that.]

[At the counter]

Me: *Hi, is there something I can help you with?*

Customer: **I need to get a copy of key made.**

Me: *Alright, do you have the key with you to make a copy of?*

Customer: **Yeah, I got it. ... ...Well... I don't have it.**

Me: *So you do or you don't have keys for this vehicle?*

Customer: **No, I've got the keys... ... I just don't know where they are.**

Me: *So you don't have any keys for this vehicle. To make a key from your VIN I'm going to need a title, a valid registration, and a valid driver's license.*

Customer: **I don't need to do all that, I just need a copy of my keys.**

Me: *Yes, you do. In order for me to make a new key for you, I'm required to have those documents.*

Customer: **But I said I got my keys, I just don't know where they are.**

[But if you have your keys, why do you need me to make you a new one?]

Me: *Hello, Parts.*

Customer: **[Garbled shouting noises]**

Me: *Hello, Parts?*

Customer: **Español?**

Me: *No.*

Customer: **Eeesspaaaaañooooool??**

Me: *No.*

Customer: **I have a '07 Audi, and I'm paying $585 per month. You just sent me a letter that says I paid too much for it.**

Me: *... Do you need to buy parts?*

Customer: **No.**

Me: *Alright, I'm going to send you to the operator. She'll find someone to help you.*

[Calls like this made me start looking for hidden cameras... and expecting Ashton Kutcher (or Allen Funt, if you're older than me) to jump out from behind the counter.]

[At the counter]

Me: *Hi, can I help you with something?*

Customer: **I need one these.**
                     [Hands me a small gas strut]

Me: *Alright, this is an unusual looking strut... What kind of vehicle is it for?*

Customer: **It's for my jukebox.**

Me: *Your... jukebox?*

Customer: **Yeah, it holds the glass up at the top.**

Me: *Got it. We don't have parts for jukeboxes here.*

Customer: **I got one here before.**

Me: *You'd be amazed how often I'm told that.*

[Does this happen to other jobs? Do people walk into PetSmart and get confused when they can't buy a refrigerator?]

[At the counter.]

Me: *Hi, is there...*

Customer: **Make me a key for my car.**
               [Drops driver's license on the counter]

Me: *Okay, do you have any keys for your...*

Customer: **I just called up here and told you all this. Make me a**
               key for my car.

Me: *Alright, in order to make a key, I'm going to need the title*
               of the vehicle, the registration, and a valid...

Customer: **I said I just called up here, and the man told me to**
               bring this receipt [tosses receipt on the counter] and
               you'd make me a key for $9.

Me: *Ma'am, I'm the only person here, and you haven't called*
               me. And this is a receipt from a different dealership.

Customer: **No, I called here, and the man told me to bring this**
               receipt and you'd make me a key.

Me: *I'll say this again, I'm the only person here, and you definitely*
               haven't called me. On top of that, I would never cut a key
               with no proof of ownership outside of a random receipt
               from another dealership. If I did that, I would be fired.

Customer: **Fuck you, you little piece of shit!**

[She tried to stomp away, but had to get a few bags of free popcorn first.]

Me: *Hello, Parts.*

Customer: **Yeah, what time are you all open 'til?**

Me: *4 o'clock.*

Customer: **Oh, do you think you all could stay open a bit later than that?**

Me: *No, I'm sorry, we close at 4.*

Customer: **Well how about you stay until 4:30 so I could come up there?**

Me: *I'm sorry, we close at 4.*

Customer: **So you ain't gonna stay open for me? That ain't right.**

[Yeah man, let me just waste another half hour of my Saturday, so you can show up, have no idea what you're looking for, and then leave with nothing.]

Me: *Hello, Parts.*

Customer: **Is this Parts?**

Me: *Yes it is, how can I help you?*

Customer: **Is this the Parts Department?**

Me: *Yes it is, how may I help you?*

Customer: **My husband wants to ask you a question.**

Me: *Okay.*

Customer: **[Hands phone to her husband] Hello?**

Me: *Yes, hello, hi. Can I help you?*

Customer: **Is this the Parts Department?**

Me: *Yes it is.*

Customer: **Alright, thank you. [Hangs up]**

[These people sounded about 80, and I think they just prank called me.]

[At the counter.]

Me: *Is there something I can help you with?*

Customer: **I need you to make us a key... for this car.
[Slides a scrap of paper with a handwritten
VIN across the counter.]**

Me: *...Okay... What sort of vehicle is this?*

Customer: **... Uh... it's a... Chevy.**

Me: *Alright, well, a key is going to be about $105.*

Customer: **Okay, yeah, that's fine. We need one right
now.**

Me: *I can get this started for you, but in order to get
into the key code system, I'm going to need to
have your driver's license. When I log into the
system, it sends the VIN and license information
to the local police, so they can have it on file.*

Customer: **[Eyes widen] Oh... uh... that's in the car.
[Both guys take off]**

*[The guy doing the talking was wearing a shirt that said "Future Billionaire"...
which seemed optimistic.]*

[... Ooooookay...]

"Yeah, I just bought a car from you all, and it's got a H and a C, and it doesn't go all the way to the middle, is that okay? because if it's not, I'm gonna bring it back to you all."

"Yeah, man, I got a '87 Monte Carlo, and I need to know how... AHHHHHHH! WHAT THE FUCK?! [running noise] There's a big 'ol snake on my car! I'mma have to call you all back."

"See, I got in an accident... well... it wasn't really an accident; my crazy psycho baby daddy smashed up my car and I need a few pieces for it."

[Chapter 6]

I'm Calling Corporate

Me: *Hello, Parts.*

Customer: **Yes, my tires are leaking gas or whatever, and I need to have you all check them out.**

Me: *Alright, let me get you out to Service and they'll get you set up.*

Customer: **Nuh uh, I just talked to them and they said I have to talk to you.**

Me: *Okay, well, this is Parts, we don't inspect tires... I'll gladly look up new ones and let you know what they cost. What size tires do you have?*

Customer: **It's '98 Lumina.**

Me: *Alright, and what size tires do you have on your '98 Lumina?*

Customer: **Excuse me?! That's your job to know, not mine.**

Me: *Okay, I just don't have that information in my catalog.*

Customer: **What do you mean you don't have the information? That's your job! I'm going to call your corporate office and have you fired!**

Me: *I wish you all the best of luck with that. [Hangs up]*

[You must be a fabulous dinner companion.]

Me: *Hello, Parts.*

Customer: **Yes, I need the repair kit for my car windows.**

Me: *Alright, what kind of car do you have, and what repair kit are we looking for?*

Customer: **It's the one for my windows! My husband said he was up there today, and you told him he needed a repair kit.**

Me: *I'm the only person here today, and I haven't spoken to anyone about a window repair kit of any sort. Could we be a bit more specific, just so I know what I'm looking for?*

Customer: **Seriously?! I just told you, I need the repair kit. It's got some wires in it, does that help you?**

Me: *So it's a window repair kit, and it has some wires in it... I honestly don't know what we're talking about right now.*

Customer: **Well maybe you need to find another job.**

[But if I found another job, I wouldn't get to talk to lovely people like you all day.]

[Midway through a call]

Customer: **Could you fax me a picture of that suspension?**

Me: *Sure, what's your fax number?*

Customer: **Uhh... hang on one sec.**
[To someone off the phone]
Hey, what's the number for our fax machine?

Voice in the background: *Fax machine? We ain't got a fax machine. Why you always askin' crazy questions like that?*

Customer: **[To me] Uhhh, I'll call you back with that.**

Me: *Hello, Parts.*

Customer: **Yeah, do you all have a solution for the fast channel removal?**

Me: *... ... ... What?*

Customer: **Do you. Have a. Solution for. The fast channel. Removal.**

Me: *That's... that's not a thing that I've ever heard of.*

Customer: **[Hangs up]**

[If you have any idea what this person meant, please get in touch.]

Me: *Hello, Parts.*

Customer: I called the headquarters and they said I could play videos on my CD player, and I need you to sell me the part so I could do that.

Me: *So you... can play videos... on your CD player?*

Customer: **Yeah, I need that part.**

[At this point, he picked up another call and conferenced us together]

Me: I'm confused. *CD players don't play videos, they only play music.*

Other guy: **Hey man, where you at?**

Customer: **[To me] Well I talked to your headquarters and they said it could. [To other guy] Hold up, I'm talking to the dealership.**

[Suddenly the phone was handed to the customer's wife / girlfriend.]

Lady: **We need the part to play movies on our CD player!**

Me: *Ma'am there are about 5 conversations happening right now, do feel free to call me back when you're finished with everyone else.*

[Unintelligible chatter from other guy, talking to someone else off his phone.]

Lady: **[To first guy] He said he ain't gonna help us.**

Other guy: *Who you talking to?*

Me: *Is this a joke? Call me back when you're finished with your other conversations. [Hangs up]*

[At the counter]

Me: *Hi, is there something I can help you with?*

Customer: **I need them fog lights for my car.**

Me: *Alright, are you just looking for bulbs, or are you trying to add fog lights to your vehicle?*

Customer: **My car doesn't have any; I want to put them on.**

Me: *[Standard make / model / VIN rigmarole]*

            Well, at this point, GM doesn't offer an add-on kit for your vehicle.

Customer: **I don't need a kit; I'll just plug 'em up in the front.**

Me: *Okay, I'll gladly order you the lamps, but that's not going to work... your car wasn't built with the necessary components and there's more to it than just plugging them in.*

Customer: **Yes it was, they're all the same, and the LTZ has 'em, so I can just plug the LTZ ones in.**

Me: *There are actually 18 different front lamp harnesses for this car, and yours is not equipped to add fog lamps.*

Customer: **Fine, then sell me the harness too.**

Me: *Okay, but that's not going to help, because you're going to need the bezels to mount the lamps into your bumper.*

Customer: **My car's already got those.**

Me: *Do they have the cutouts to mount fog lamps?*

Customer: **Well no, they're solid.**

Me: *Alright, then you're going to need the bezels too. Do you have a switch to turn them on and off?*

Customer: **Yeah, I already got the switch.**

Me: *Have you changed the stock switch? Because the fog lamp switch is integrated into the headlamp switch, and according to your VIN, your vehicle has the standard switch.*

Customer: **Okay, fine, then sell me the switch too.**

Me: *Absolutely. The lamps, bezels, harness, and switch come to $775 with tax; these parts are non-returnable, and I can't guarantee that any of it will work.*

Customer: **$800? No man, you're not talking any sense. I saw one online for $50. I'm just gonna get that one. [Walks away]**

[This is why there are different trim levels... if you buy the cheapest one, you can't expect it to have the features of the most expensive one... unless you're this guy.]

Me: *Hello, Parts.*

Customer: **You were supposed to call me months ago and you never did!**

Me: *Ma'am, I don't call people, I just order parts. Is there something that I can help you with?*

Customer: **Tell me if my recall parts are there!**

Me: *[Standard info gathering... Who are you? What are you talking about? Etc.]*

         Looks like there isn't anything on order for you, because all of your open recalls have been handled.

Customer: **Well then what is this recall to change the ignition cylinder and keys?!**

Me: *... It's a recall where we change your ignition cylinder and replace your keys, but it's already been taken care of.*

Customer: **You think that was cute?! Because that's not fucking cute! Put some else on the fucking phone!**

Me: *Ma'am, that's exactly what we do in that recall, but if you'd like to talk to my manager, he'll be in at 10 on Monday.*

Customer: **Oh, yeah, fucking of course he's not there. Is this really how you treat people?!**

Me: *It's how I treat people who act like you. [Hangs up]*

Me: *Hello, Parts.*

Customer: **Good morning. I have a Mitsubishi, and I know you can't help me, but I need my car reprogrammed, and I was wondering if you could help me.**

Me: *I can't help you. You need to go to Mitsubishi.*

Customer: **So you can't help me? I should probably go to Mitsubishi.**

Me: *That would be your best bet.*

[I know you can't help me, but can you help me?]

Me: *Hello, Parts.*

Customer: **1-2-5-8 5-3-2-8, you got one'a them?**

Me: *...Yes, I appear to have one of those in stock.*

Customer: **Is that a common problem?**

Me: *Is... me having parts in stock... a problem?*

Customer: **No man, with this car. Is that a common problem with this car?**

Me: *I picked up the phone and you read a part number at me... I don't know what kind of car you have. I don't know what the part is. And there's no way I could know what kind of problems you're having.*

Customer: **Man, why you actin' like that?!**

     [Sets phone down and starts having a conversation with someone else about broccoli...]

Me: *Hello? ... ... Hello?*

     [I left the call on speaker for a minute while I helped out one of the techs, and then I hung up. A few seconds later, the phone rings again.]

Me: *Hello, P...*

Customer: **You ain't never told me if you got one! Do you have one?!**

Me: *You read me a part number and I said I had it in stock.*

Customer: **Man, you're a asshole. [Hangs up]**

[At the counter]

Me: *Hello, can I...*

Customer: **MAP sensor.**

Me: *Alright. For what kind of...*

Customer: **Cruze.**

Me: *Year?*

Customer: **[Exasperated sigh] '12.**

Me: *Okay, do you happen to have the last 8 digits of your VIN? There are four options on these.*

Customer: **Who brings their VIN number?! Just give me the part I need.**

Me: *Well, see, your VIN would eliminate all of these other options and I could make sure I was getting you the right part.*

Customer: **Yeah? Well if it's so important, what's your VIN?**

Me: *D4143669.*

Customer: **Man, why you gotta have a attitude like that? What are you, the boss's son or something? Just give me my part.**

Me: *I need your VIN to verify the correct part. I don't want to guess, I want to get it right the first time.*

Customer: **Fine. I'll go get it.**

[Did you honestly think the person who spends 10 hours a day asking people for VINs wouldn't know their own?]

Me: *Hello, Parts.*

Customer: **I need the coolant recipe.**

Me: *...Okay... What sort of car do you have?*

Customer: **Uhhh... What kinda cars do you make that start with 'C'?**

Me: *... Well, we make the Cobalt, Cavalier, Camaro, Corvette, Cruze, Caprice, Corsica...*

Customer: **You said Cruze, right? I think that's what I got.**

Me: *Alright, and we're looking for the... what?*

Customer: **I need the coolant... residue.**

Me: *The coolant... reservoir?*

Customer: **Yeah, that sounds like my problem. How much is that?**

Me: *Hello, Parts.*

Customer: **My car has a blerp.**

Me: *...I have no idea what that means.*

Customer: **It means I need a new AC compressor.**

Me: *Of course it does. What sort of car do you have?*

Customer: **It's a '02 Grand Am.**

Me: *And it has a... blerp?*

Customer: **Yeah, what can you tell me about the blerp?**

Me: *I... I... I have no familiarity with this word.*

Customer: **Well there should be a new part number to fix the blerp.**

Me: *Okay... I only see one part number for the compressor and it's $690.*

Customer: **To fix a blerp? No, you ain't looking at the right thing.**

Me: *I don't think I'm going to be able to help you.*

[Again, if you have any idea what this person was talking about, do get in touch.]

\

Me: *Hello, Parts.*

Customer: **I bought a Camaro a few years back, and I want those stickers that go on the side.**

Me: *Alright, there are a bunch of different decals for the sides. Which ones are you looking for?*

Customer: **I want those three that go at the back.**

Me: *The three gills on the rear quarter? I don't stock anything like that, but I could order them.*

Customer: **Yeah you do; you stock 'em. I want the chrome ones.**

Me: *I definitely don't stock those, and according to my catalog, they're only available in black.*

Customer: **Why you lying to me? I know you got 'em there. I'm gonna come up there and get some.**

[Well, you would obviously know more about my stock than I would...]

Me: *Hello, Parts.*

Customer: **I need to buy that screw that holds the seat down.**

Me: *To the floor?*

Customer: **Yeah, they're universal for all the models.**

Me: *Okay... What kind of car do you have?*

Customer: **It's a '84 Caprice.**

Me: *According to my catalog, that part is no longer available.*

Customer: **Do they have seats in the new cars?**

Me: *Yes, of course they do.*

Customer: **Well they all use the same screw as my car.**

Me: *No, they definitely don't use the same parts as an '84 Caprice.*

Customer: **That's bullshit.**

Me: *Hello, Parts.*

Customer: **Yeah, I need a part.**

Me: *You've found the right place. What kind of part are you looking for?*

Customer: **Well, all I know is it stretches. Do you have one of those?**

Me: *It... stretches?*

Customer: **Yeah, it connects two parts together and it stretches.**

Me: *...Okay... Well, let's start with what kind of car you have.*

Customer: **Oh... uh... you know what, I'm gonna have to call you back with that.**

[If it wasn't obvious, this person was looking for a transmission shift cable.]

Me: *Hello, Parts.*

Customer: **I was referred to you all for an actuator.**

Me: *Well, there are a lot of actuators in a car. Can we start with what sort of vehicle it is?*

Customer: **I own the car.**

Me: *That's always a plus, but I really need a make and model to look anything up in my catalog.*

Customer: **Man, I don't know. There's a actuator in there and it's making a loud noise, and they said you had it.**

Me: *There's a good chance that I do, but without knowing what kind of car you have, there's just no way for me to look this up.*

Customer: **Forget it, I'll just call someone else.**

Me: *Hello, Parts.*

Customer: **Yes, I need a motor, do you have that?**

Me: *Alright, what sort of car do you have?*

Customer: **Ohhhhhh, I don't know, I just need a motor.**

Me: *Like... an engine?*

Customer: **Yeah. How much does that cost?**

Me: *Anywhere from $2000 to $30,000 depending on what engine you need.*

Customer: **Well I just called up there and they said it was $85.**

Me: *For an engine? The thing under the hood that makes the car move?*

Customer: **Yeah, that's what you all just told me.**

Me: *That's not... that's not possible. There's clearly some miscommunication here. Can we start from the beginning, with what kind of car you have?*

Customer: **None of y'all there know what you're talking about.**

Me: *Hello, Parts.*

Customer: **Do you have the assembly in stock?**

Me: *Do I have... the assembly... in stock?*

Customer: **Yeah, the assembly, you have that in stock?**

Me: *I... I...*

Customer: **Oh shit, how the hell are you supposed to know what I'm talking about if I don't tell you what I need? I'm sorry man, I need a headlamp assembly for a '07 Impala; passenger side.**

Me: *Ohhhh, that assembly.*

Customer: **Yeah, I don't know how the hell you was supposed to know that.**

[Moment of clarity.]

153

[Midway through a call]

Me: *Those are about $73 + tax. They'd need to be payed for in advance before I can get them on order.*

Customer: **Why you making me come there and pay for parts I don't need?!**

Me: *Excuse me?*

Customer: **If this is how you all treat people, I'm going to go buy it somewhere else.**

Me: *I gave you a price on a part that you asked me for... I'm not making you buy anything.*

Customer: **[Hangs up]**

Me: *Hello, Parts.*

Customer: **This is the dealer, right?**

Me: *It certainly is, how can I help you?*

Customer: **Alright, you should be able to help me. I've got a '79 Buick Regal, and I put a '68 Olds 400 rocket motor in it, and I need all of the gaskets.**

Me: *...All of the gaskets?*

Customer: **Yeah, I just need all of the gaskets to put that engine in that car.**

Me: *Okay, I don't have any information about putting 1968 engines into 1979 cars.*

Customer: **But you're the dealer.**

Me: *I am, yes... but my catalog doesn't have any information about doing engine swaps in 50-year-old cars.*

Customer: **So you're telling me that you're not going to help me?!**

Me: *I do not have the information that you're looking for. Your best bet is either going to be a shop that works on vintage cars, or the internet.*

Customer: **Well thanks for nothing. [Hangs up]**

[I wish the catalog was even 10% as good as people seemed think it was.]

[At the counter]

Me: *Hi, is there something I can help you...*

Customer: **What is this?**

                 [Points to a display of accessories next to the counter]

Me: *I think that's a cross rail for a roof rack.*

Customer: **Well I don't like people who think! I like people who know! [Walks away]**

Me: *Alright, I guess I'm done here.*

[Well, you're in luck, because I do know that I hate you.]

Me: *Hello, Parts.*

Customer: **My radio isn't working.**

Me: *Alright, how can I help you?*

Customer: **You the Parts guy, you gotta tell me what's wrong! What do I need to fix it?**

Me: *Well... from the information I have, I'd say... you need a new radio?*

Customer: **No man, the radio cuts on, but it ain't working.**

Me: *This sounds like something that you need to speak to Service about.*

Customer: **So you ain't gonna tell me what I need to fix it?**

Me: *Sir, I just look up parts. There's no way I can diagnose a problem like this over the phone.*

Customer: **Well it sounds like you need to find a new job!**

Me: *You have a great rest of your day. [Hangs up]*

[Looking back, I really should have taken this guy's advice sooner.]

Me: *Hello, Parts*

Customer: **I lost my keys, and I need to get a new one made.**

Me: *Okie doke, what kind of car do you have?*

Customer: **It's a 2003 Pontiac Grand Prix**

Me: *Alright, well, those keys have a security chip in them, and I would need to have the car here to get the new key programmed. I can get you to Service and they can help arrange a tow.*

Customer: **Oh, I don't need a tow, I can just drive it up to you all.**

Me: *No you can't, you have no keys, remember?*

Customer: **Oh yeah, you're right. I can't drive that car anywhere.**

Me: *Let me get you to Service, they'll get you set up.*

[After spending 15 agonizing minutes figuring out what this person needed]

Customer: **I'm just going to buy it on Amazon. Let me get that part number.**

Me: *No.*

Customer: **What do you mean, no?**

Me: *The word is pretty self explanatory.*

[It means, "get fucked." Go call Amazon's Parts Department and see where that gets you.]

Me: *Hello, Parts.*

Customer: **How much does this part number cost? [Gives part number]**

Me: *Looks like that is $329 + tax. I have one in stock.*

Customer: **Give me a discount.**

Me: *No. The price is the price.*

Customer: **Well, I asked for a discount, so you have to give it to me.**

Me: *No, the world doesn't work like that. And you didn't ask for anything, you demanded it.*

Customer: **I'm gonna come up there and get one, and you better give me a discount. [Hangs up]**

[I eventually got to a point where I would practically give things away if the person acted with any common courtesy.]

[Chapter 7]

Why Is This So Difficult?

Me: *Hello, Parts.*

Customer: **Alright, I've got a conundrum.**

Me: *Okay...*

Customer: **So, see, I just bought an '84 Fiero with no keys, and I need...**

Me: *No.*

Customer: **No?**

Me: *I can't make keys for a vehicle that old.*

Customer: **Man, that's what all the other dealerships keep telling me.**

Me: *Correct, that's because our system doesn't have key codes for cars of that age.*

Customer: **Why is this so fucking difficult?!**
                 [Hangs up]

[Better question is, why the hell did you buy an '84 Fiero with no keys?]

Me: *Hello, Parts.*

Customer: **I got a '07 and I need the harness and the kit.**

Me: *Okay, you have an '07... what? And which harness and kit are we looking for?*

Customer: **Oh my god. How do you not know this?! Do you have any idea what you're doing?!**

Me: *As a matter of fact I do. [Hangs up]*

Me:	*Hello, Parts.*
Customer:	**How come my car doesn't have a second row mat?!**
Me:	*I honestly don't know.*
Customer:	**I just bought the car from you, and I want to know why my car doesn't have a second row mat!**
Me:	*Okay, this is Parts... it sounds like you need to speak to your salesman.*
Customer:	**I talked to them, and they say it doesn't come with. How is that possible?!**
Me:	*I honestly don't know. Stop by the Parts Department and we'll try to get everything worked out for you.*
Customer:	**No! You need to help me right now!**
Me:	*There's no way that I can put a set of mats in your car over the phone. If you come to the Parts Department, we will do our best to remedy this situation.*
Customer:	**That's it, I'm done with you. [Hangs up]**

[One sec, let me just fire up the parts teleporter real quick...]

Me: *Hello, Parts.*

Customer: **You need to put some fluid in my car.**

Me: *Okay... what?*

Customer: **I have an '08 Equinox and someone on the internet told me that only the dealer can put power steering fluid in it.**

Me: *No, you can definitely do it. The reservoir is on the right side of the engine; there's a big black cap with a steering wheel on it.*

Customer: **No! That's not right! The internet said that only the dealership can do it! It's a special system!**

Me: *Okie doke... Let me get you to the Service Department, perhaps they'll be able to help you.*

[Well if someone on the internet said, it MUST be true...]

[At the counter]

Me: *Hi, is there something I can help you with?*

Customer: **I need you to make me a valet key.
             [Hands me a key and $5]**

Me: *We don't make valet keys... I can make you a
             copy of this key, but it's $30.*

Customer: **No man, I just called up here and the other
             guy told me a valet key was $5.**

Me: *Well, I'm the only person here, and I've received
             no calls about valet keys.*

Customer: **I don't like you lying to me. Just make me a
             valet key. [Pushes key and $5 toward me]**

Me: *Alright, I'll try again... We don't make valet keys. I
             can copy this key for you, but it's going to be $30.*

Customer: **Where's your manager?! I'm going to tell him
             that you're lying to customers.**

Me: *Again, I'm the only person here. The manager will
             be in at 8 on Monday.*

[I feel like all I need to say about this is... Saturday...]

Me: *Hello, Parts.*

Customer: **I need to get a price on a rim.**

Me: *[Standard make / model / VIN questions]*

               Alright, that rim is $461 + tax. I would have to order it.

Customer: **I didn't want a price on four, I just want a price on one!**

Me: *That is the price for just one rim.*

Customer: **Well, I don't want it with the tire or anything! I just want one rim!**

Me: *Alright, I'll say it again, that is the price for one rim.*

Customer: **It is?! Your prices are crazy! [Hangs up]**

Me: *Hello, Parts.*

Customer: **I bought a car from you a few weeks ago, and you still need to give me my second key!**

Me: *Okay, I can check to see if I still have the extra. What name was the vehicle purchased under?*

Customer: **[Shouts name at me]**

Me: *I don't seem to have that name in my system. Could it be purchased under a different name?*

Customer: **You guys just keep giving me the run around. I'm just going to bring the car back! I shouldn't be treated like this!**

Me: *I'm sorry ma'am... I just don't have your name in my system anywhere.*

Customer: **I bought it three weeks ago from [local dealership]! This is crazy! Is this how you treat your customers?**

Me: *Ma'am, that's a completely different business. We are an independently owned and operated franchise. We have no affiliation with that dealership.*

Customer: **What's your name?! I'm going to call your corporate office and tell them how you're treating people!**

Me: *My name is Josh. What you need to do is call the dealership you purchased the car from and speak to your salesman or a manager.*

Customer: **This is ridiculous! [Hangs up]**

[Part of me wishes that these people all did call GM, and somewhere there's an entire filing cabinet specifically dedicated to my apparent mistreatment of people.]

[At the counter]

Me: *Hi, is there something I can help you with?*

Customer: **I need four tires.**

Me: *Alright, what size tires are you looking for?*

Customer: **I don't know.**

Me: *...Okay, do you happen to have your VIN?*

Customer: **No.**

Me: *Alright, I'm really going to need to know one of those in order to get the right tires.*

Customer: **Forget it! I'm never coming back here again! [Stomps away]**

[But if you never come back, how will we ever stay in business?! Oh wait.]

[Midway through a call]

Me: *That part is $161.00 plus tax, it's something I would have to order.*

Customer: **Well, I was hoping it would be more like $40.**

Me: *Okay.*

Customer: **So you all'll sell it to me for $40?**

Me: *No, the price is $161.00 plus tax.*

Customer: **Why's it so expensive?**

Me: *I don't know. The prices are set by GM.*

Customer: **Put your manager on the phone, he'll sell it to me for $40.**

Me: *He'll be in tomorrow at 8 AM, but I promise you he's not going to sell it to you for $40 either.*

Customer: **Well I'm gonna call him in the morning and have a talk with him.**

Me: *Yup, I wish you all the best of luck with that.*

[Yeah man, and I'm hoping my commission check is going to be for a million dollars this month.]

[At the counter]

Me: *Hi, is there something I can help you with?*

Customer: **I need some parts for my truck.**

Me: *Alright, what sort of truck do you have?*

Customer: **I think it's an '07, 3500 Silverado.**

Me: *Would you happen to have the VIN, so I can make sure I get all of the correct setups for this vehicle?*

Customer: **No, I don't have that... but it's in your shop for service right now.**

Me: *[Look the VIN up in the computer]*
           Okay, so you have a 2005, 1500 Express van.

Customer: **Ohhhhh, is that what it is?**

[These two vehicles are quite different from each other, right? I'm not the crazy one, right?]

Me: *Hello, Parts.*

Customer: **I ordered a part two days ago, and the man said it would take three days to come in.**

Me: *...Okay.*

Customer: **So, is it there yet?**

Me: *No, shipping takes three days, and it's only been two. It'll be here tomorrow.*

Customer: **Alright, fine. [Hangs up]**

[Repeat that first thing you said, and then stop and think about it for a second.]

Me: *Hello, Parts.*

Customer: **Do you have anything for Alice May?**

Me: *Perhaps, what part is on order?*

Customer: **It's a limitation... valve.**

Me: *A... limitation valve?*

Customer: **Yeah, for a Malibu.**

Me: *And it's a... limitation valve?*

Customer: **Yeah, a limitation valve.**

Me: *I don't have that name in my system.*

Customer: **Alright, I'm on my way down to get it.**

[At the counter. Finishing an order.]

Me: *Can I get a name to put on this?*

Customer: **Davis.**

Me: *Alright, give me one second, I'll get you a ticket for this, and you'll be ready to go.*

                    [Brings the bill to the counter]

Customer: **Why does it say Davis on here? My name is Reeves.**

Me: *...One minute ago, I asked you for a name to put on the order, and you told me to put Davis on it.*

Customer: **I never said that.**

Me: *Of course... Please take the bill to the cashier, and I'll fix this on our end.*

[And I'll give you one guess what name they gave when they came to pick it up...]

[At the counter]

Me: *Hi, is there something I can help you with?*

Customer: **You called me this morning and said my part was in, and I need to pick it up.**

Me: *Alright, I'm the only one here today, and I haven't called anyone. What name were the parts ordered under?*

Customer: **No, you called me and said they were in. Here's my receipt.**

     [Hands me a receipt from a dealership about 80 miles west]

Me: *Alright, this is from a completely different dealership.*

Customer: **I know. I ordered the parts from them, but I want to pick them up here, because this is closer to my house.**

Me: *...Unfortunately, it doesn't work like that. They are the ones who called you. Your part is waiting for you at that dealership.*

Customer: **But I don't want to go out there. I want to pick it up here.**

Me: *Well, I can order you one and have it here on Tuesday, but you're going to have to pay for it.*

Customer: **But I already paid for it!**
[Waves receipt at me]

Me: *I understand, but you paid for it at that dealership, and we have no affiliation with them.*

Customer: **Then what am I supposed to do?**

Me: *You need to drive to that dealership and pick it up.*

[Who knew it was such a difficult concept that you had to pick something up at the same place you ordered it...]

[At the counter]

Me: *Hi, is there something I can help you with?*

Customer: **I need this part right here.**
              [Points to a picture in an owner's manual]

Me: *Alright, what kind vehicle is this for?*

Customer: **[Flips manual over] It's a 2010 Impala.**

[Look up the part, bill it out, send the customer on their way. 20 minutes later, he's back.]

Me: *Is there something I can help you with?*

Customer: **This part doesn't fit on my car.**

Me: *Well, there's only one option for a 2010 Impala, and that's it.*

Customer: **But it doesn't fit.**

Me: *Okay, do you have the car here? Could we get the VIN and make sure we have all of the right information.*

Customer: **Yeah, it's out in the lot.**

Me: *Alright, let's go have a look.*

[Walk with the customer out into the lot.]

Customer: **It's that one, right there.**

Me: *The Malibu?*

Customer: **Yeah, that's my car.**

Me: *...Okay... So you have a 2008 Malibu, not a 2010 Impala.*

Customer: **Well, it's all the same, it just has a different body on it.**

[If they were the same, then wouldn't the part have fit? And why do you have a manual for a 2010 Impala when you have a 2008 Malibu? Let me guess, the manuals are all the same?]

[At the counter]

Customer: **I need to return this, 'cos you sold me the wrong part earlier!**

Me: *You said you wanted a front pinion seal. You pointed to it in the picture, and said, "I want the front pinion seal." So I got you a front pinion seal.*

Customer: **Oh... y-you remember that?**

Me: *Yes. Yes I do.*

Customer: **...Well alright, then I guess it's not the wrong one.**

Me: *Hello, Parts.*

Customer: **Can I come up there and get a free car wash?**

Me: *You certainly can, as long as you have our license plate frame on your car.*

Customer: **Well, what if I've got a state trooper plate on my car?!**

Me: *Then you're going to have to speak to the Service Department.*

Customer: **[Hangs up]**

[We (internally) referred to our car wash as "the scratch machine," but people would still queue up for it... because it was free...]

[At the counter]

Customer: **I'm just checking to see if my parts are in.**

Me: *Okay, what's your last name; I'll have a look.*

Customer: **Uhh... ... ...**

Me: *Your last name? It's the only way I'm going to be able to find anything.*

Customer: **It's uh... ... uhh....**

[Sifts through their wallet for a minute... Holds out their driver's license at me...]

[Not knowing what car you own is one thing. Not knowing your own last name is an entirely different level.]

Me: *Hello, Parts.*

Customer: **Your driver was just here and the part he dropped ain't the right thing. He dropped off a GMC logo, and we need the Chevy bow tie.**

Me: *Okay, do you have the last 8 digits of the VIN so I can look this up again?*

Customer: **No, I don't have that. I'm on the toilet right now.**

Me: *Seriously? How about you call back when you're a bit less indisposed. [Hangs up]*

[This shop called all the time, and this was positively classy for them...]

[At the counter]

Customer: **Gimme that part number.**

Me: *We don't give out part numbers.*

Customer: **Yes you do.**

Me: *Oh, well, you would certainly know more about our policies than I would.*

Customer: **So let me get that part number.**

Me: *We don't give out part numbers.*

Customer: **Well that's bullshit.**

Me: *Hello, Parts.*

Customer: **Hey Parts, you're going to need the last 8 digits of my VIN aren't you?**

Me: *Almost certainly.*

Customer: **Well, I don't have that. I'll call you back. [Hangs up]**

[If you knew I was going to need it, why did you call and... you know what, forget it.]

Me: *Hello, Parts.*

Customer: **I was driving down the highway yesterday, and that plastic piece blew the fuck up.**

Me: *It blew up?*

Customer: **Yeah, it blew up.**

Me: *Alright... what kind of car do you have, and what plastic piece are we talking about?*

Customer: **Man, I don't know how else to describe it.**

Me: *So it's a plastic piece... and it blew up?*

Customer: **Yeah, well, it didn't explode or anything, it just blew up.**

Me: *Ah... Do you have a VIN, or any real information for me to go on?*

Customer: **Oh... I'll have to call you back with that.**

[If you have a guess at what this person was talking about, feel free to send it to jwellingtonparts@gmail.com. Note: you will NEVER get it.]

[At the counter]

Me: *It looks like this is something that I would have to order.*

Customer: **Well, I need it today.**

Me: *According to my locator, the nearest dealership that stocks one is about 850 miles away. I would have to order it.*

Customer: **Alright, I need it today.**

Me: *I understand, but I would have to order it. I can have it here on Tuesday.*

Customer: **But you said that other dealership had one. Why can't you send someone to get it?**

Me: *I'm sorry, I can't send someone 1700 miles to pick up a part for you. I have one option, and that is to order the part and get it here on Tuesday.*

Customer: **Well, what am I supposed to do?**

Me: *It seems like there are two options... You can go on a 30-hour road trip, or you can order it from me.*

Customer: **...Well, I guess I'll just order it.**

[It's a shame that our parts teleporters have the reliability of a McDonald's ice cream machine.]

[... Really?]

"That's 's' as in 'dollar sign'."

"Yeah, how much would it cost for you all to diagnostify my car?"

"If I gave you a wrong part number, how is that my fault?"

"You mean you're not going to send my parts because I bounced **one** check?"

[Chapter 8]

Thanks For Nothing

Me: *Hello, Parts.*

Customer: **Yes, I have a van, year 1987, and I need the repair kit.**

Me: *What sort of repair kit are you looking for?*

Customer: **For the back.**

Me: *Alright... what exactly does this repair kit fix?*

Customer: **It fixes the back.**

Me: *Okay, what in "the back" does it fix?*

Customer: **If you don't know what I'm talking about, I'll just call someone else who does.**

Me: *I think that's going to be your best bet.*

Customer: **Thanks for nothing. [Hangs up]**

[Glad to be of assistance.]

Me: *Hello, Parts.*

Customer: **I got a question about a '93 Chevy GMC.**

Me: *Okay.*

Customer: **So?**

Me: *So... what?*

Customer: **What size is it?!**

Me: *What size is... what?*

Customer: **I just asked you! What size is it?!**

Me: *...Well, it's a truck, so I assume it's... big?*

Customer: **Forget it. [Hangs up]**

[Ver. Batim. What the hell was I supposed to say?]

Me: *Hello, Parts.*

Customer: **Yeah, I have a 2004 Buick GT.**

Me: *A what?*

Customer: **It's a '04 Buick GT.**

Me: *Are you sure? ... Because that's not a car.*

Customer: **What do you mean, am I sure?**

Me: *Is there any chance I could get the last 8 digits of your VIN?*

Customer: **Ugh, fine.**

[Eventually returns with his VIN]

Me: *So you have a 2007 Pontiac Grand Prix.*

Customer: **Whatever, they're all the same.**

[Yes... your fictitious car is definitely the same as a real car.]

Me: *Hello, Parts.*

Customer: **I have a '09 HHR and I need the light switch.**

Me: *Okay, which light switch are we looking for?*

Customer: **It's that gray one where you plug the bulbs in.**

Me: *Alright... where is it in the car?*

Customer: **I just said it was in the...**

     [Mid sentence, the boyfriend grabbed the phone.]

Customer: **I called the parts store, and they said they didn't have one.**

Me: *They didn't have... a gray switch in the front where you plug the bulbs in?*

Customer: **Yeah, up by the headlight.**

Me: *Do you need a... headlight socket?*

Customer: **Man, fine. Call it whatever you want.**

[Fine, I'll call it Susan.]

Me: *Hello, Parts.*

Customer: **I need the actuator.**

Me: *Okay. What sort of car do you have, and what actuator are we talking about?*

Customer: **I already changed one.**

Me: *...Okay. There are a lot of actuators in a car, could we be a bit more specific?*

Customer: **Well I need the other one.**

Me: *The other one? Can we please start with what kind of car you own?*

Customer: **I just need the other one.**

Me: *We've established that, but unless you tell me what kind of car you own, and which actuator you're looking for, I'm not going to be able to help you.*

Customer: **I already told you that! I changed the one, but now I need the other one.**

[Oh oh oh, the OTHER actuator. Let me just type that into my catalog really quick and see what it comes up with.]

Me: *Hello, Parts.*

Customer: **I have a '06 Monte Carlo, and I need a new radio.**

Me: *Do you happen to have the last 8 digits of your VIN, so I can see which radio you have?*

Customer: **Well, I don't need a new one. I went to the junkyard and bought one from a '08 Malibu, and I need to know if that'll work in my car.**

Me: *From what I see in my catalog, there are no 2008 Malibu radios that will work in your car.*

Customer: **Well what if I got one from an Impala?**

Me: *Those probably aren't going to work either.*

Customer: **Then what am I supposed to do?**

Me: *Well, for starters I would recommend getting a radio from a Monte Carlo.*

Customer: **Oh... well I guess that makes sense.**

[And yet here we are...]

Me: *Hello, Parts.*

Customer: **I need to get a rudder.**

Me: *A rudder? Cars don't have rudders.*

Customer: **Yeah it does; it's got a rudder on the engine.**

Me: *Okay, what sort of car are we working with, and where on the engine might this rudder be?*

Customer: **It's a '08 Malibu, and it's in that piece on the top.**

Me: *It's... in that piece... on the top?*

Customer: **Yeah man, you know, it's that rudder on the top of the engine.**

Me: *Is there any chance we're talking about an intake manifold tuning valve?*

Customer: **A what? No man, it's just the rudder!**

Me: *Alright, I just don't have any listings for rudders in my catalog. If you'd like, you can come in and look at a few pictures and maybe that'll help us find the right part.*

[And the part he needed was... An intake manifold tuning valve... sensing a trend? It's almost like I knew what I was talking about.]

[Closing a conversation]

Me: *We can definitely get these for Tuesday; just let me know before Monday at 3.*

Customer: **Alright. Love you, honey.**

Me: *... Uhhh, thanks?*

Customer: **Ohmagod. [Hangs up]**

[It's nice to feel appreciated once in a while.]

Me: *Hello, Parts.*

Customer: **Yeah, is this Hollywood?**

Me: *Yes it is, how can I help you?*

Customer: **Hollywood, I don't normally do this, but you a real good lookin' guy, you single?**

Me: *I am, yes... This doesn't sound like a parts related inquiry.*

Customer: **Oh... uh... well, I'm gonna bring my car up there tomorrow, you gonna be working?**

Me: *...Yes. I'll be here.*

Customer: **Well, I guess I'll see you then.**

[This call happened about 2 minutes after this gentleman left the counter.]

[Two days later]

Me: *Hello, Parts.*

Customer: **Yeah, is this Hollywood?**

Me: Ugh... yes it is... How can I help you?

Customer: **Hey Hollywood, I called you the other day.**

Me: *Yes. I know.*

Customer: **What time you get off work today? I was thinkin' we could go get a drink, and maybe grab dinner.**

Me: *No, that's okay.*

Customer: **Oh, well what if I came by there to see you?**

Me: *I would be glad to assist you with any parts-related inquiries.*

Customer: **Alright, well, I'm gonna come up there and see you.**

[I was mysteriously absent when he showed up.]

[Open the counter Saturday morning... there's a guy staring at me]

Me: *Good mor...*

Customer: **Valve cover gasket.**

Me: *Okay, for what sort of car?*

Customer: **[Immediately gets on his phone and walks away]**
               [5 minutes later he's back]

Me: *Did we find out...*

Customer: **Are they both the same?**

Me: *You still haven't told me what kind of car it's for.*

Customer: **[Gets back on his phone and walks away]**
               [5 minutes later he's back]

Me: *So, do we know what kind of car we have?*

Customer: **How much are they?**

Me: *Okay... We're still missing an important piece of information... What kind of car do you have?*

Customer: **[Gets back on his phone and walks out of the building]**

[Why? Just... why? What was the point of even showing up?]

Me: *Hello, Parts.*

Customer: **I need a door speaker for a '06 Cobalt.**

Me: *Alright, those look like they're $36 + tax.*

Customer: **Pass. [Hangs up]**

[You're welcome.]

[At the counter]

Me: *Hi, is there something I can help you with?*

Customer: **Do you have that round thing for my car?**

Me: *... What?*

Customer: **That round thing. For my car. Do you have it?**

Me: *That round thing? How could I possibly know what you're talking about?*

Customer: **Well, I ordered it the other day.**

Me: *Okay, so you're here to pick up a part.*

Customer: **Yeah, that round thing.**

Me: *Yes... we've established that.*

[Thankfully, there's only one round thing in a car...]

[At the counter]

Me: *Hi, is there something I can help you with?*

Customer: **I lost that clicky thing for my car, and they said you could tell me what it costs.**

Me: *Okay, what kind of car do you have?*

Customer: **[Hands me a title]**

Me: *Alright, this is a Chrysler.*

Customer: **Uh huh. I need that clicky thing that unlocks my doors.**

Me: *Well, I can't look up parts for Chryslers.*

Customer: **Why not?**

Me: *...Because this is a Chevrolet dealership?*

Customer: **It is?**

Me: *Yup, the big signs with the gold bow tie, and the hundreds of Chevys parked in the lot didn't give that away?*

Customer: **Oh, I didn't even look.**

[Two huge signs, hundreds of cars, every employee with a monogrammed gold bow tie on their shirt, the wall full of Chevy signs behind the counter... it's easy to miss.]

Me: *Hello, Parts.*

Customer: **I need a new radio.**

Me: *Okay, what kind of car do you have?*

Customer: **Do I have to get one from you or can I just get one at Best Buy?**

Me: *You can do whatever you'd like; it's your car.*

Customer: **Fuck you. [Hangs up]**

[Okie doke.]

Me: *Hello, Parts.*

Customer: **I need to get a new radio for my car.**

Me: *Alright, and what sort of car do you have?*

Customer: **It has a single exhaust.**

Me: *So, we need a radio for a car with a single exhaust?*

Customer: **Yeah, mine doesn't work anymore.**

Me: *I'm going to need a VIN to look this up.*

Customer: **You can't just give me a ballpark figure?**

Me: *... Okay... A single exhaust radio looks like it's probably around $400...*

Customer: **Alright, that's all I needed to know.**

[*You lucked out, those dual exhaust radios are pretty pricey.*]

Me: *Hello, Parts.*

Customer: **Yes, I need to get some suspension parts for my car.**

Me: *Okay, could we start with the last 8 digits of your VIN.*

Customer: **How many?**

Me: *I need the last 8 digits of the VIN.*

Customer: **How many is that?**

Me: *It's 8. I need the last 8 digits of the VIN.*

Customer: **Well... uh... how many is that?**

Me: *...It's 8? Count to 7 and then go one more than that... that's 8.*

[You know that one that looks like a friendly little snowman? I need that many.]

Me: *Hello, Parts.*

Customer: **Hello Parts, I have a '01 Suburban, and I just bought a marginator for it, but I don't know where it goes.**

Me: *You bought a... what?*

Customer: **A marginator. I think it's under the hood somewhere. Could you tell me how to install it?**

Me: *I think you're going to have to speak to Service. Hang on, I'll switch you out there.*

[I would imagine you just find the old marginator, unhook it, and then put the new one in its place... but I see how that could be difficult, since a marginator isn't a thing.]

Me: *Hello, Parts.*

Customer: **I need a bypass.**

Me: *... Okay... for what sort of car?*

Customer: **Well, it's some kind of van.**

Me: *Alright, I need a VIN for this vehicle.*

Customer: **Antifreeze.**

Me: *Yeah, that's not a VIN.*

Customer: **You can't tell me what it's gonna cost?**

Me: *At the very least, I need to know what kind of car it is.*

Customer: **It's got coolant in it.**

[It carried on like this for three phone calls... at which point we finally found out it was a Ford...]

[At the counter]

Me: *Hi, is there something I can help you with?*

Customer: **THAT LADY JUST CAME FROM THE BACK!**

Me: *... ... ... What?*

Customer: **[Points at me] That lady!**

Me: *I'm sorry, there are no ladies back here.*

Customer: **Man, this place makes no sense. [Walks away]**

[Yeah man, at least we can agree on that...]

[A Visit to the Parts Department]

'Twas the Saturday before Christmas, and all day at work,
The counter was flooded with nothing but jerks.

"These parts are all wrong!" They'd often exclaim,
"It's almost as if you were born without brains!"

"My apologies, sir" I would say with a grin,
"I'll check them again, can I please get your VIN?"

"That's out on the car," they'd say with much strife,
"I've never been treated so poor in my life!"

"I do understand," I'd say with a start,
"It's just without that, I can't find the right part."

"Now listen to me, you part-selling slob!"
"Perhaps you should go and find a new job!"

I'd bite back my tongue, but oh how I'd yearn
To shout, "get out of my store and never return!"

But I'd smile and nod and keep it inside,
It's best just to take these people in stride.

"Do you know what it's called, or where it might go?"
"Aren't you the Parts guy?! The hell don't you know?!"

"Let's start with the car, make, model, and year."
"Get me your manager, bring him right here!"

"You might help me out — give me some information,"
"And maybe this wouldn't cause so much frustration."

"That's it, I'm done here, you boneheaded hack!"
"I'm leaving this place, and not coming back!"

The saddest part is, this trend isn't recent...
Why is it that people can't seem to be decent?

[December 19, 2015]

[Chapter 9]

What's Your Last 8?

[Caller ID shows it's the oil change shop down the street]

Me: *Hello, Parts.*

Customer: **Uh... how much oil goes in this car?**

Me: *... I don't know... What kind of car do you have?*

Customer: **... ... Uh... Where does it tell me that?**

Me: *Really? It should say all over the vehicle, or hopefully on your paperwork...*

Customer: **It's a... uh... C... 5... uh... 5... 0... ... 0...**

Me: *Okay, it's a C5500 truck? I'm going to need the VIN to get correct fluid capacities for a truck that large.*

Customer: **This is Chevy, right?**

Me: *It is, yes.*

Customer: **And you don't know how much oil goes in your cars?**

Me: *Your job is exclusively to change oil in cars, right?*

Customer: **Uhh...**

Me: *And you don't know how much oil to put in cars? I don't have any information for you. [Hangs up]*

Me: *Hello, Parts.*

Customer: **[To someone off the phone] Shut up, man, I'm calling the dealership.**

Me: *Hello, Parts.*

Customer: **Hey parts, I need a suspension bolt for a '98 Cavalier.**

Me: *[VIN? No. Any useful information? No.]*

Alright, I don't have any of those in stock. I could ord...

Customer: **What do you mean you don't have any in stock?! But you're the dealership! Just go out where you build the cars and get one!**

Me: *...You do realize we don't build cars here, right? This is a dealership... And even if we did, we definitely wouldn't be building 17-year-old Cavaliers... Now, we could order these bolts and have them for you on Tuesday.*

Customer: **No man, forget it. [Hangs up]**

[Seriously, what is it about the people who call on Saturdays?]

Me:	*Hello, Parts.*
Customer:	**Yeah, I just bought a car and I need to get a manual for it.**
Me:	*Alright, what sort of car are we talking about?*
Customer:	**It's a 1989 Lumina.**
Me:	*... .... And you need a manual for it?*
Customer:	**Yeah, it's not safe driving without it.**
Me:	*[Under my breath] It's probably not safe to drive in the first place...*
Customer:	**Excuse me?!**
Me:	*Oh, I said my manual printer doesn't seem to stock these anymore; you're probably going to have to find something out on the internet.*
Customer:	**Well how am I supposed to drive it until I find one?**
Me:	*Just like any other car? You don't need a manual to drive... It doesn't make your car any more or less safe...*
Customer:	**...Alright. [Hangs up]**

[This person called about this a lot, and they were constantly claiming that we needed to give them a loaner until we got them a manual... because it was somehow our fault.]

Me: *Hello, Parts.*

Customer: **Hi, this is [name] from [local shop].**

Me: *... Hi.*

Customer: **Why do you always sound so down whenever I call?**

Me: *Because you only ever call for free information.*

Customer: **Come on, don't be like that! You know that's not the way it is.**

Me: *Alright, how can I help you?*

Customer: **Well... I just need to know what suspension codes this truck's got. I'm trying to get some aftermarket shocks, and they say there are different codes.**

Me: *... Huh, sounds like free information to me.*

Customer: **Come on, I just need you to help me out. I get all my parts from you!**

Me: *Mmhm, cards on the table, you've done about $28 of business with us this year... which, I'll admit, is better than the $3 of business you did with us last year.*

Customer: **...You know, I think I'm going to call someone else.**

Me: *I think that would be lovely.*

[This shop called almost every day... and sometimes multiple times in a day...]

Me:	*Hello, Parts.*
Customer:	**Need brakes for a Silverado.**
Me:	*Alright, can I get the last 8 digits of your VIN, so I can get the right brake setup?*
Customer:	**No. I already told you everything you need. I need brakes for a Silverado.**
Me:	*Okay... the Silverado has been in production for 18 years and each model year has had dozens of variations. I'm going to need your VIN so I get the specific setup for your vehicle.*
Customer:	**I already told you! Are you going to help me or what?!**
Me:	*I don't really know any other way to say this... unless you give me the last 8 digits of your VIN, there's no way for me to get the right parts for your vehicle.*
Customer:	**Man, you are rude as hell! I'm never calling you again! [Hangs up]**

[Jeremy Clarkson voice: Oh no. Anyway.]

Me: *Hello, Parts.*

Customer: **I broke my key in my ignition and you
             need to make me one from my VIN
             number.**

Me: *Well, before I can do anything, you're going
             to need to supply me with three things: the
             title or original bill of sale, your valid
             registration, and your valid drivers license. All
             documents need to have matching names
             and addresses.*

Customer: **Who the fuck carries their title?! Fuck
             you, asshole. [Hangs up]**

[Quick and to the point; my kind of customer.]

Me:	*Hello, Parts.*
Salesperson:	**Hi! Is the Parts manager there?**
Me:	*Nope.*
Salesperson:	**Is he going to be back soon?**
Me:	*I honestly don't know.*
Salesperson:	**Alright, does he have a fax line? I have some great offers that I'd like to tell him about.**
Me:	*He doesn't, no.*
Salesperson:	**Alright, does he have an email address that I could send these to?**
Me:	*No, he fears technology.*
Salesperson:	**Okay, does he have a voice mail, so I could leave him a message?**
Me:	*No, he refuses to set it up.*
Salesperson:	**Well... when's he going to be back?**
Me:	*Could be a week, could be a month for all we know... he just kinda walked out... for all I know, I'm the manager now.*
Salesperson:	**Would you like to hear about our offers?**
Me:	*Not really, sorry.*
Salesperson:	**I'll try back on Tuesday, maybe he'll be back by then.**
Me:	*I sure hope so. I don't have any idea what I'm doing here.*

[Messing with sales calls was one of my few sources of joy.]

[At the counter]

Me:	*Alright, that fluid is $9.28 per quart.*
Customer:	**No it isn't.**
Me:	*It absolutely is. [Shows him the price.]*
Customer:	**No. It isn't. I bought some here three or four years ago, and it wasn't that much.**
Me:	*I understand, but the prices do change.*
Customer:	**No they don't. That's not how much it costs.**
Me:	*Well, you'd certainly know better than I would.*
Customer:	**You're ripping me off.**
Me:	*Sir, I am not; it's $9.28 per quart. You can go to any GM dealership in the country and that's the price it will be.*
Customer:	**You're ripping me off.**
Me:	*Okay. Well, I just checked and I don't have any in stock, so I'm not going to be able to help you. This is a standard specification fluid, you can get it at any parts store, it's all exactly the same.*
Customer:	**No, it's not the same. I want the GM fluid.**
Me:	*Alright, well it's $9.28 per quart, and I don't have any; you're going to have to go to a different dealership.*
Customer:	**You're ripping me off.**
Me:	*I'm not, and I'm not helping you anymore.*

[You're right, man, no company has ever increased the price of a product before...]

Me: *Hello, Parts.*

Customer: **Quick question, I have some sort of Saturn and I need to get a spare key for it. How much does that cost?**

Me: *Alright, what sort of Saturn do you have?*

Customer: **It's like a '05 or an '08 or something. I don't really know.**

Me: *Do you at least know what model it is? That might narrow it down for me.*

Customer: **Oh... uh... no, I don't really know what it's called.**

Me: *Do you have access to the car?*

Customer: **Yeah, it's out in the garage.**

Me: *Could you have a look and let me know?*

Customer: **Oh... well... You know what, I don't need a spare key, mine is fine. [Hangs up]**

[?]

Me: *Hello, Parts.*

Customer: **My friend bought a spoiler up there a couple years ago, and I want to get that same spoiler.**

Me: *Alright, and what sort of spoiler are we talking about?*

Customer: **Look him up. His name is, uh... Erwin... Police Officer.**

Me: *His last name is... Police Officer?*

Customer: **No, that's his job. Can't you look him up by his job?**

Me: *Uhh... no, that's not how my system works.*

Customer: **Oh, I'll have to call you back.**

[Yeah man, we keep a full, constantly updated list of our customers' occupations... you know, for when we can't remember someone's name, but we do remember they worked at Wendy's in 2006.]

[At the counter]

Me: *Hi, is there something I can help you with?*

Customer: **I need three copies on the engine.**

Me: *... Pardon me?*

Customer: **You need to give me three copies on the engine.**

Me: *I have no clue what we're talking about.*

Customer: **[To a guy getting popcorn, who we'll call "Three Copies"] Hey! What's that engine?**

Three Copies: *Tell him you need three copies!*

Me: *Guys, you need to tell me what you're talking about or I'm not going to be able to help you. What sort of car do you have? What "on the engine" am I supposed to be giving you three copies of?*

Customer: **How do you do the chains?**

Three Copies: *We need three copies.*

Me: *... Okay. Are you looking for a parts explosion? A diagram of the chains for a car? What kind of car do you have?*

Customer: **Yeah, up on the engine!**

Three copies: *Make sure you give us three copies.*

Me: *Alright... I suppose I'll just guess.*

Me: *Hello, Parts.*

Customer: **How much is that seal at the back?**

Me: *...Alright, the seal at the back of what? Let's start with what kind of car you have.*

Customer: **Oh, it's an old Corvette... maybe a '96?**

Me: *Okay, do you have the last 8 digits of the VIN?*

Customer: **The what?!**

Me: *The VIN? It's the serial number of the car. It should be on your insurance, or your registration, or on a little plate on the driver's side of the dash... I just need the last 8 digits.*

Customer: **How about... [reads about 30 random letters and numbers]**

Me: *Okay, that's definitely not a VIN. I just need you to read me the last 8 digits of it.*

Customer: **Do you read left to right or right to left?**

Me: *... ... Left to right. We read left to right. Please read the last 8 digits from left to right.*

Customer: **Hmmmmmmmm... ... left to right... ... I'm going to have to call you back then. [Hangs up]**

Me: *Hello, Parts.*

Customer: **Do you have those wires?!**

Me: *Excuse me?*

Customer: **I NEED THE WIRES THAT GO TO THE SHIFTER!!**

Me: *Alright... for what sort of car?*

Customer: **Impala. You know what, I'm just gonna blow the mother fucker up for the insurance.**

Me: *Okay.*

Customer: **So how long would it take to get those wires?! Like next year or something?!?!**

Me: *...What? That connector would take a day to order. If you came by tomorrow, before 4, and got it on order, we'd have it on Saturday.*

Customer: **This is fucking ridiculous.**

Me: *Alright. [Hangs up]*

Me: *Hello, Parts.*

Customer: **[Sounds like they're across a room] Hello?**

Me: *Yes, hello.*

Customer: **[A few steps closer] Hello??**

Me: *Hi. Hello... Parts.*

Customer: **[A few steps closer] Hello?? Are you there??**

Me: *Yes. Hello. Parts department. How can I help you?*

Customer: **How many points are on my card?**

Me: *... Excuse me?*

Customer: **I need to know how many points are on my card!**

Me: *Alright... this is a Chevrolet dealership.*

Customer: **No, I called the casino.**

Me: *No, this is definitely a Chevrolet dealership.*

Customer: **Well, that's not who I called. [Hangs up.]**

[At the counter]

Me: *Hi, is there something I can help you with?*

Customer: **Do you have a Service manager?**

Me: *We do, but he's out today. He'll be back in on Monday.*

Customer: **Well I need to file a complaint. I brought my car in because my power steering is acting up, and they're trying to tell me that I have to pay to get it fixed.**

Me: *Well... that's how Service works... It's not free... it costs money to get your car fixed...*

Customer: **I called your headquarters and they said I didn't have to pay, and I want to file a complaint!**

Me: *Alright... I just look up parts; I'm not really going to be able to do anything for you.*

Customer: **What's your name?**

Me: *I'm Josh. You really need to take this up with Service, there's literally nothing I can do about this.*

Customer: **You aren't helping me at all! I'm going to get you in trouble too!**

Me: *Alright, you have a great time with that. [Walks away]*

[Did you infer what day of the week this was?]

[At the counter]

Me: *Hi, is there something I can help you with?*

Customer: I need... I need the belt for a '05. A '05... uh... an '05... an '05 uh... '05... uhhh... that one that starts with an 'E'... a uh... an '05... Altima!

Me: *Well... that's a Nissan.*

Customer: Oh, wait, that's my wife's car. My car is that '05... uh... it's that '05 that starts with an 'E'... El...antra!

Me: *The Elantra is made by Hyundai. Would you like to keep guessing?*

Customer: Yeah, I'm gonna figure it out, gimme a minute... it's a '05... a '05 uhhh... Envoy!

Me: *Hey, that's actually a car we make! What belt are you looking for?*

Customer: I need the serpentine belt.

Me: *Alright, what engine do you have in there?*

Customer: ... Uh... it's that one that's shaped like an L.

Me: *I don't think we make motors that are shaped like L's...*

Customer: Wait... not an L, it's a V6.

[First customer of Saturday morning, at the counter]

Me: *Hi, is there something I can help you with?*

Customer: **Yeah, I have a 2009 Hyundai Sonata, and I need a lug nut and stud for it.**

Me: *I'm sorry, I can't get parts for Hyundais.*

Customer: **Well this is Parts isn't it?**

Me: *Correct, but this is a General Motors dealership... We only sell parts for GM vehicles.*

Customer: **[Aggressive sigh] So you don't have anything for my car?**

Me: *Correct. Your best bet is either going to be a Hyundai dealership or a parts store.*

Customer: **[Walks away]**

[A minute later, the phone rings]

Me: *Hello, Parts.*

Customer: **I have a '03 Econoline, that real long one, and I need to get those oil lines up on the engine.**

Me: *You have a Ford Econoline?*

Customer:	**Yeah, it's the long one.**
Me:	*Well, this is a Chevrolet dealership, so unfortunately I'm not going to be able to help you out.*
Customer:	**But this is the Parts Department, right?**
Me:	*It is, yes... but this is Chevrolet... we can't get parts for Fords here.*
Customer:	**[Grumbles] [Hangs up]**

[Very next phone call]

Me:	*Hello, Parts.*
Customer:	**Hi Parts, if I give you a VIN number, can you tell me what kind of Scion this is?**
Me:	*[Head on desk] I'm sorry, this is a Chevrolet dealership... My system can't decode Scion VINs...*
Customer:	**So you can't tell me what sort of Scion it is?**
Me:	*Nope, you'll need to call either Scion or Toyota.*
Customer:	**Oh... Well, I guess I'll have to go call Scion or Toyota. Thanks. [Hangs up]**

["Think of how stupid the average person is, and realize half of them are stupider than that." - George Carlin, describing every minute of my work day.]

Me: *Hello, Parts.*

Customer: **I need the button on the handle.**

Me: *... Okay, well... let's start with what kind of car you have.*

Customer: **Ugh, I just told you, I need the button on the handle.**

Me: *Yes, I know... but to look anything up, I need to at least know what kind of car you have.*

Customer: **2016 Camaro.**

Me: *Thank you. What button on what handle are we looking for?*

Customer: **Oh my god, I have to tell you three times?! I need the button on the handle.**

Me: *Okay... do you have the last 8 digits of your VIN? I have 96 options for handles on this vehicle.*

Customer: **L.T.**

Me: *That's not a VIN. I need the last 8 digits of your VIN so I can be sure I'm getting the correct information for you.*

Customer: **Is there anyone else there who knows what they're doing?**

Me: *Nope, it's just me here tonight.*

Customer: **[Hangs up]**

[At the counter]

Me: *Hi, can I help you with something?*

Customer: **Yeah, I need half a bottle of transmission fluid.**

Me: *Alright, well, I don't have half bottles, but I can sell you a whole one.*

Customer: **...But I only need half.**

Me: *I understand, but unfortunately I can't sell half of a bottle of fluid.*

Customer: **Well, sell me the whole thing at half price. I don't need a whole one.**

Me: *I'm sorry, I can't do that.*

Customer: **Why not? I only need half.**

[At the counter]

Me: *Hi, can I help you with something?*

Customer: **How much is that Corvette hat over there?**

Me: *With tax, the hats are $15.81.*

Customer: **Hmmmmm... ... ... $15.81, you say?**

Me: *Yes, they're $15.81, with tax.*

Customer: **And that's the price with tax?**

Me: *Yes. That is the price with tax.*

Customer: **Alright, I'll take it.**

Me: *Alright, give me one second.*
[Gets hat and bill]
Take that to the cashier and you'll be all set.

Customer: **[Looks at the invoice, confused] Why do I have to pay for it?**

Me: *Pardon me?*

Customer: **Well, I don't think I should have to pay for this.**

Me: *Okay... well... that's kinda how this works.*

Customer: **But I bought a Corvette from here, so shouldn't I get a hat for free?**

Me: *You just bought a Corvette?*

Customer: **Well, I bought it back in 2006... and they didn't give me any free things when I got it.**

Me: *Well, unfortunately, this wasn't even the same company in 2006.*

Customer: **So, you're still gonna make me pay for the hat?**

Me: *I am. Yes.*

Customer: **Alright, I don't want it anymore.**

[...]

Me: *Hello, Parts.*

Customer: **Hello, Parts, you gotta help me out.**

Me: *Alright, what can I do for you?*

Customer: **I need a tail pipe for a 1986 Pontiac Parisienne.**

Me: *Uh... a what?*

Customer: **It's a 1986 Pontiac Parisienne with a 262, and I need the tail pipe for it.**

Me: *Yeah, that's not going to be available anymore.*

Customer: **What do you mean it's not available? Did you even look?**

Me: *I didn't. But it's a part for a 30-year-old Pontiac that was only made for 4 years... Let me have a look... Alright, according to my catalog that part was discontinued 17 years ago.*

Customer: **Well, I need you to order it for me.**

Me: *I would love to, but like I said, GM discontinued the part 17 years ago... There are none in our warehouses, and no dealership in the country has one in their inventory.*

Customer: **So put the order in, and they'll make a new one for me.**

Me: *What? That's not how it works, they don't produce one-off parts for 30-year-old cars...*

Customer: **I don't understand why you're giving me such a hard time about this. I just need you to order me a tailpipe.**

Me: *Again, this part hasn't been available for nearly two decades... I'm sorry, but unless you have a time machine that can take us back to 1999, there's just no way that I'm going to be able to help you with this.*

Customer: **You know, fine, you're no help at all. I'm going to take my business somewhere else.**

Me: *Well, I wish you all the best of luck.*

[I actually wish you horrible luck.]

[... Honestly?]

"Yeah, I got a A-u-r... something... and I need that thing... that thing... that puts stuff on your windows."

"That's great, but I'm not going to use any of your parts, I'm going to bring my own."

"If I... uh... wanted to be a mechanic here, do I... uh... have to... you know... be a mechanic?"

[Chapter 10]

Are You Kidding Me?!

[First call of Saturday morning... Sensing a trend yet?]

Me: *Hello, Parts.*

Customer: **I need a e38 PCM.**

Me: *... Okay... would you happen to have a VIN for this vehicle, so I can look this up?*

Customer: **No. I don't need a fucking VIN, I just need a e38 PCM.**

Me: *Alright, it's just that I can't look up an "e38 PCM." I need a VIN for the vehicle; that's how my catalog works.*

Customer: **Are you fucking kidding me with this shit?**

Me: *No. I don't kid. Especially not at 8:05 Saturday morning.*

Customer: **So you just don't have any fucking clue what you're doing, do you?**

Me: *[Hangs up]*

[I assume this guy's Saturday to-do list reads: 1 - Harass the kid at the local car dealership. 2 - Chill.]

Me: *Hello, Parts.*

Customer: **I need you all to make me a key for my car, and I've got aaallll the ID you want.**

Me: *Okay, I'm going to need to have the title, registration, and your drivers license.*

Customer: **Oh, well I don't have any of that.**

Me: *Then I won't be able to assist you.*

Customer: **But I've got a bunch of other things with my name on them.**

Me: *Unless there's a title, registration, and license among them, I won't be able to assist you.*

[Well you're in luck, just bring us your Blockbuster Membership Card and your Frequent Sandwich Eater Card from Jimmy John's, and we'll knock that key right out for you.]

Me: *Hello, Parts.*

Customer: **My car is making a clucking noise on the side.**

Me: *Clucking?*

Customer: **Yeah, what part is that?**

Me: *It's clucking? ... Clucking is the sound a chicken makes.*

Customer: **Yeah, it's clucking on the side. What part does that?**

Me: *It would probably be best to have a tech check it out.*

Customer: **But I just need the clucking part on the side. Can't you look that up for me?**

[Maybe it was the... wishbone...]

[Midway through a conversation]

Me: *Well, it doesn't look like I have any in stock, but [local dealership about 20 miles away] has them today if you need them in a hurry.*

Customer: **Alright, I'll be by your place in about 15 minutes, will you have them picked up by then?**

Me: *...What?*

Customer: **You said that other place had them.**

Me: *Correct, they have them, but if you want them, you're going to have to pick them up from them.*

Customer: **But why would I pick them up?! That's your job!**

Me: *Unfortunately, my driver is loaded today, and there's no way we're going to be able to do that.*

Customer: **Then why did you tell me they had them?! This is no way to run a business. [Hangs up]**

[How incredibly disrespectful of me... to tell you the quickest way to get the part that you're clearly in a hurry for...]

Me: *Hello, Parts.*

Customer: **Yeah, I need that transmission that you have all those problems with.**

Me: *Okay... and which transmission would that be?*

Customer: **You know, that enclosed one.**

Me: *What? Let's start with what sort of vehicle you have.*

Customer: **It's a Chevy.**

Me: *Unfortunately that doesn't narrow it down much... any chance you have the last 8 digits of your VIN handy?*

Customer: **No, I don't have that. I just need that enclosed one.**

Me: *[Eventually gets enough useful information to look it up. It's a wiper transmission]*

                  Looks like that's about $125 + tax.

Customer: **Is that the shop price?**

Me: *Are you with a shop?*

Customer: **No, but I bought my car from a dealer.**

Me: *Okay... so you're not with a shop?*

Customer: **No. [Hangs up]**

[At the counter]

Me: Hi, can I help you with something?

Customer: **I need to pick up a part I ordered.**

Me: Alright, do you have your receipt?

Customer: **I don't have that. I ordered it a couple weeks ago.**

Me: [Gets name. They don't remember what they ordered]

Well, I don't show anything on order for you this month. Are you sure you have something on order?

Customer: **What's the date today?**

Me: It's the 26th of March*.

Customer: **Hm, well, I think I ordered it in... October, maybe?**

Me: Okay... October isn't 'a couple weeks ago'... that's 5 months ago... and it looks like the only activity for you since last October was an oil change.

Customer: **Well, I know I ordered it, do you still have it?**

Me: We don't even know what kind of part you ordered... as far as I can see, the last time you ordered something was an axle, and that was in June of 2015.

Customer: **Yea! That's it! I need to pick that up.**

Me: Alright, let me see if we still have one.

Customer: **Actually, you know what, I have some other things I want to do today, so I'll just come back another day. [Walks away]**

[*2016]

[At the counter]

Me: *Hi, can I help you with something?*

Customer: **I need this. [Drops an oil-covered chunk of metal on the counter]**

Me: *Ooookay, and what exactly is that?*

Customer: **I don't know, just go in back and match one up for me.**

Me: *Unfortunately, it doesn't work that way; you're going to have to tell me what vehicle it's for... and what exactly it is.*

Customer: **Well, I don't know any of that. Get me the manager! He'll match it up for me.**

Me: *I am the manager. I'd love to help you, but without some more information, I'm not going to be able to help you.*

Customer: **Then get me a different manager who'll match it up for me.**

Me: *There aren't any other managers; it's just me.*

Customer: **But you're not going to match it up for me.**

Me: *Correct. Until you get me the information I need, we will not be able to assist you.*

Customer: **This is ridiculous. [Walks away]**

[I wasn't the manager...]

Me: *Hello, Parts.*

Customer: Yeah, I have a 1913 Impala.

Me: *Uh...*

Customer: Wait, no, it's a 2013.

Me: *That sounds more likely.*

Customer: I also have a '96 Monte Carlo, and I need the code.

Me: *Alright, what code are we looking for.*

Customer: The code to put that radio in that other car.

Me: *So... an unlock code? Is the radio locked?*

Customer: No, the radio's unlocked. I just need the code to put it in the other car.

Me: *You're putting the radio from a '96 Monte Carlo into a '13 Impala? I don't think you can just swap those...*

Customer: I know! That's why you need to give me the code!

Me: *I'm sorry, I just don't know of a code that does that.*

Customer: Send me to Service! They'll know.

Me: *Absolutely. Hang on a second.*

[Midway through a call]

Me: *That's only six digits; I need the last 8.*

Customer: **I just gave you eight!**

Me: *Could you read them to me again, please?*

Customer: **53. 20. 43.**

Me: *... Okay, that's still only six numbers.*

Customer: **No, that was eight.**

Me: *Alright... Well, can you read me the two things that come before those?*

Customer: **So you want ten numbers?**

Me: *... I guess...*

Me: *Hello, Parts.*

Customer: **I need a [yelling to someone off the phone] What's it called?!**

Voice in the Background: *Platinum gasket!*

Customer: **I need a platinum gasket.**

Me: *Okay, for what kind of car?*

Customer: **It's a 1 1 1.**

Me: *That's not a car. Do we know what kind of car it is?*

Customer: **Oh lord... [yelling to someone off the phone] He wants to know what the car is called!**

Voice in the Background: *Just tell him you need a platinum gasket!*

Me: *Yes, I hear that... It's just that I can't look up a platinum gasket for a 1 1 1... I need like... a real car and a real part.*

Customer: **...You know what, I'll just have him call you; he knows what he's talking about.**

[Why do I doubt that?]

Me: *Hello, Parts.*

Customer: **I just got a letter that says my car isn't safe to drive.**

Me: *A recall notice? Do you have the recall number?*

Customer: **I guess. Let me read what it says to you. [Starts reading the whole notice]**

Me: *No... I just...*

Customer: **[Continues reading]**

Me: *I just... I just need...*

Customer: **[Continues reading]**

Me: *The recall number...*

Customer: **[Finishes reading]**
Was it in there somewhere?

Me: *No... I just need the 5-digit recall number. It's usually near the top, in bold.*

Customer: **Hmmmm, well, let me read it to you again. [Reads whole notice]**

[Midway through a conversation]

Me: *That's not something that I stock, but I could order it.*

Customer: **How long would it take?**

Me: *It's stocked at a far away warehouse, so it would be three business days.*

Customer: **What does that mean?**

Me: *...It means that it's going to take three business days to get here.*

Customer: **Well, get it for me tomorrow. I need it tomorrow.**

Me: *I understand, but it's going to be three business days... and since tomorrow is Sunday, and Monday is a holiday, the earliest we can get one is next Thursday.*

Customer: **Fine, where's the warehouse that it's at? I'll just pick it up myself!**

Me: *Well, it's in Rancho Cucamonga, California, and they don't sell to the general public.*

Customer: **...So I'll have it on Thursday, if we order it today?**

Me: *Correct.*

Customer: **Alright, order it.**

Me: *Hello, Parts.*

Customer: **I have an '07 Aveo. Do you have that piece with the bushing?**

Me: *Potentially... What sort of piece is it?*

Customer: **It's... something to do with the wheels.**

Me: *Alright.*

Customer: **That's the best I can describe it.**

Me: *Is it in the front or the rear?*

Customer: **I don't know... I figured you would know.**

Me: *Hello, Parts.*

Customer: **The other guy said I needed the last 8 digits of my VIN. I'm looking for some bolts.**

Me: *Alright, excellent. What's your last eight?*

Customer: **6 3 B.**

Me: *Yeah, that's not 8 digits.*

Customer: **How about 6 3 B 3?**

Me: *Nope, you're still missing four digits.*

Customer: **I'll call you back. [Hangs up]**

[Hold up all the fingers on one hand, and 3 more on the other. I need that many.]

251

Me: *Hello, Parts.*

Customer: **How much are tires?**

Me: *It depends on the size and the brand.*

Customer: **[Aggressive sigh] The normal ones!**

Me: *I'm sorry, there aren't normal ones...There are tons of different sizes.*

Customer: **Then the ones for a '08 Trailblazer!**

Me: *There are a bunch of different sizes that fit that car. I really just need the size... it's right on the side of the tire.*

Customer: **I'm up there all the time, and you don't know what size tires go on my truck?!**

Me: *We don't keep that information on file...*

Customer: **Well you just lost a customer!
[Hangs up]**

[It's adorable when people think that saying we've "lost a customer" makes me feel anything other than joy, knowing that there's one less moron I might have to deal with.]

Me: *Hello, Parts.*

Customer: **I was looking online, and I want to get a Z28 bowtie for my car.**

Me: *Cool, do you have a Z28?*

Customer: **No.**

Me: *Well, the parts for those are restricted, and you have to have the car to order them.*

Customer: **That's bullshit! I can order whatever I want!**

Me: *For the most part, yes... but this is an uncommon car, and many of the parts, including the hollow bowtie, are restricted.*

Customer: **It doesn't matter, that car is stupid anyhow. They should have never made it. It's got stupid wheels, and it's ugly, and...**

Me: *Is there anything else I can help you with?*

Customer: **Well... while I've got you on the phone... I need the emblem for an '03 Blazer.**

[An '03 Blazer is basically a 2015 Z28 Camaro... they're almost impossible to tell apart.]

Me: *Hello, Parts.*

Customer: **I got a tire.**

Me: *Okay...*

Customer: **So how much is that?**

Me: *How much is... what? Do you need a price on a tire?*

Customer: **No, I've already got the tire.**

Me: *... Okay... How can I help you?*

Customer: **How much did it cost?**

Me: *That should be on your receipt?*

Customer: **Oh yeah... Thanks. [Hangs up]**

[It was that number the cashier lady said before you gave her money.]

[Caller ID shows a Service Writer is calling]

Me: *Hello, Parts.*

Writer: **Josh, can you hear what's playing on the radio right now?**

Me: *... Uhh... no?*

Writer: **It's Olivia Newton-John. This might be one of the most beautiful songs ever written.**

Me: *Did you just call me to tell me Olivia Newton-John was on the radio?*

Writer: **... ... ... Maybe.**

Me: *Alright, I'll come out there are listen to it.*

Writer: **You won't regret this.**

[Here's to you, Bobby Lew. You're the only person from this place that I miss.]

[At the counter]

Me: *Hi, is there something I can help you with?*

Customer: **Do you have this part? [Points to number on an emissions printout]**

Me: *That's not a part, that's your odometer reading.*

Customer: **So you don't have it?**

Me: *Well, no, that's not a part...*

Customer: **Oh... Where does it say what part I need?**

Me: *It doesn't. You're probably going to have to have it checked out in Service.*

Customer: **Then why'd they give me this paper? [Walks away]**

Me: *Hello, Parts.*

Customer: **What size are the connections?**

Me: *Pardon me?*

Customer: **I've got a 3500 truck and I need to know what size the connections are.**

Me: *[VIN? / What are you talking about? / Etc.]*

                 Alright, and what connections are you trying to find the size of?

Customer: **Oil cooler.**

Me: *Unfortunately, I don't have those sizes in my catalog.*

Customer: **Are you fucking kidding me?! Then how do your mechanics know what tools to use?!**

Me: *... I suspect they just line them up with their various sockets and wrenches... They don't come ask me for dimensions for every bolt they remove...*

[Well, except for that one tech... that I'm sure everyone has in their shop... whenever I'd see him coming, I would pray for the phones to ring, so someone else could deal with him...]

[Chapter 11]

I Want to Talk to Your Manager

Me: *Hello, Parts.*

Customer: **I bought a car from you two days ago, and the battery went dead.**

Me: *Okay, I'm sure that's covered under your warranty. If you brought the car in, we could replace it for you.*

Customer: **I already bought a new one, and I just need to get reimbursed.**

Me: *Alright., did you buy it from us, over the counter?*

Customer: **No, I bought it from a store in Tennessee.**

Me: *Well, then there's not much I can do for you. If you had brought it to any Chevrolet dealership, they would have been able to fix it under your warranty.*

Customer: **So you're not going to reimburse me?!**

Me: *I'm sorry, that's not something that I'll be able to do.*

Customer: **Put your manager on the phone!**

Me: *He'll be in on Monday at 8.*

Customer: **[Hangs up]**

Me: *Hello, Parts.*

Customer: **Is this Parts?**

Me: *Yes it is. How can I help you?*

Customer: **Okay parts, the man said I need the bank and the sentinel.**

Me: *You need the... what?*

Customer: **The man told me I need [papers shuffling] the bank... and the sentinel.**

Me: *I'm sorry, I don't know what either of those are; cars don't have sentinels, and a 'bank' just indicates which side of the engine something is on. Can we start with what sort of car you have?*

Customer: **Oh.. I don't know; that's just what the man wrote down. He said to call you and you would know what I need.**

[10 minutes before closing on a Friday.]

Me: *Hello, Parts.*

Customer: **I have a customer here who needs a part in a hurry.**

Me: *Okay, what sort of vehicle are we looking at?*

Customer: **Well, it's a 2012 Ford Focus.**

Me: *Alright, well, this is a Chevrolet Dealership, so I'm not really going to be able to assist you.*

Customer: **The customer says it has the same 4.3 V6 as a 2002 Express van, and I need a starter for it.**

Me: *I don't know a whole lot about cars, but I'm confident Ford never put a Chevy van engine into the Focus.*

Customer: **Well, I need to get a starter for this car in a hurry, what am I supposed to do?**

Me: *I would recommend calling Ford. They probably have more access to Ford parts than I do.*

Customer: **But the part I need is a Chevrolet part.**

Me: *For a Ford? Alright, that starter is about $500 + tax, and I would not be able to accept a return in this situation.*

Customer: **Oh... maybe I'll call Ford then.**

[If you are the owner of one of these van-engined Focuses, get in touch; I would like to go for a ride.]

[At the counter]

Me: *Hi, can I help you?*

Customer: **I need a part.**
             [Drops receipt on the counter]

Me: *Alright, looks like that's right here.*
             [Literally on the shelf next to the counter]

Customer: **I should get a discount for my inconvenience.**

Me: *Excuse me? You've been here less than 30 seconds.*

Customer: **I want to talk to your manager.**

Me: *He'll be in on Monday. Did I do something wrong?*

Customer: **You guys screwed up big time! Where's the manager?! I want to file a complaint.**

Me: *Alright, he'll be in on Monday, but I still have no idea what's wrong.*

Customer: **Well we're gonna come back on Monday and complain in person!**

Me: *Okay, we'll be looking forward to it.*

[Disappointingly, he never showed up. I honestly wanted to hear the complaint.]

Me: *Hello, Parts.*

Customer: **I've got a 2013 Malibu and I need the Eco.**

Me: *Alright... What are we looking for again?*

Customer: **I need the Eco. It's in the trunk.**

Me: *... There's an Eco nameplate on the trunk... Is that what you're looking for?*

Customer: **Does that control the Eco?**

Me: *No... it's just a badge.*

Customer: **Well, he just told me to call and ask for the Eco in the trunk.**

Me: *Hello, Parts.*

Customer: **I need a price on a bumper cover.**

Me: *Okay, for what sort of car?*

Customer: **I don't know, I just need a price.**

Me: *Alright, do you have the last 8 digits of your VIN?*

Customer: **Fuck no, the car isn't here.**

Me: *Well, see, it's hard to give you a price if you can't tell me what sort of vehicle it's for.*

Customer: **Ugh, fine.   It's a Monte Carlo, single exhaust.**

Me: *Thank you.*

Customer: **Actually, here, I have a VIN. [Reads VIN]**

Me: *Okay, this VIN is for an Impala with dual exhaust.*

Customer: **Whatever man, they're all the same!**

[Yeah, you're right... those two things are definitely the same... how stupid of me.]

[At the counter]

Me: *Hi, can I help you with something?*

Customer: **I need to pick up a part for Marilyn.**

Me: *Alright, just picking something up? You said the name was Marilyn?*

Customer: **Yeah, it's for Marilyn.**

Me: *Cool, what's the last name?*

Customer: **... Last name?**

Me: *Yeah... the last name that part was ordered under? You said it was Marilyn...?*

Customer: **... uhhh... yeah, 200,000 miles.**

Me: *What?*

Customer: **Yeah, 200,000 miles. Marilyn Muffler.**

[For anyone outside of the Chicagoland area, Merlin Muffler and Brake, or Merlin 200,000 Mile Shop, is a chain auto repair shop.]

Me: *Hello, Parts.*

Customer: **I just bought a Camaro and I'm allergic to the seats.**

Me: *Alright... How can I help you?*

Customer: **I need the other seats.**

Me: *The... other seats?*

Customer: **Yeah, for the people who are allergic to the normal ones.**

Me: *... ...That's... not a thing.*

Customer: **What do you mean?! What are you supposed to do if you're allergic to the seats?!**

Me: *I honestly don't know. I've never encountered this before.*

Customer: **Well find me someone who has!**

Me: *Gladly, let me get you out to the Service Department.*

[It's gotta be a weird doctor's appointment when you find out you're allergic to... seat.]

[At the counter]

Me: *Hi, can I help you?*

Customer: **[On their phone. Pushes a part at me.]**

Me: *... Hi. Can I help you?*

Customer: **[Still on their phone. Angrily pushes part at me.]**

Me: *Yeah, I'm not sure what that means. Is there something I can help you with?*

Customer: **[To the phone] My god, hold on.
                 [To me] I NEED ONE OF THESE!**

Me: *Sure. Would you happen to have your VIN?*

Customer: **NO. I JUST NEED ONE OF THESE!**

Me: *Without a VIN, I can't help you.*

Customer: **[To the phone] This guy is an idiot.
                 [Walks away]**

[I blame the 5G.]

Me: *Hello, Parts.*

Customer: **Alright, here's the deal, my check engine light is on. So I put some sensor on it, but the check engine light is still on, and they said I need to go to you and have a reciperator or something put on it.**

Me: *... Okay...*

Customer: **So are you going to fix my car or what?!**

Me: *I think you're going to need to speak to Service.*

Customer: **Oh my god, I'm so sick of having to explain this to people! [Hangs up]**

[At the counter]

Me: *Hi, can I help you with something?*

Customer: **Need a module for a '95.**

Me: *Alright, what kind of module are you looking for? Do you have the last 8 digits of your VIN?*

Customer: **Naw, that's on the car. See, here's the thing, the car is missing.**

Me: *The car is missing?*

Customer: **Yeah, the car is missing.**

Me: *Like... you don't know where it is?*

Customer: **Naw, like it's not idling right. What module is that?**

Me: *Can we be any more specific? What kind of car is it? What sort of module are we looking for?*

Customer: **Man, I don't have time for this. [Walks away]**

Me: *Hello, Parts.*

Customer: **I've got a ... ... uh... '16 Trax.**

Me: *Alright.*

Customer: **What color is it?**

Me: *... I don't know, it's your car.*

Customer: **Well, what's the paint code?**

Me: *I'm going to need the last 8 digits of your VIN.*

Customer: **The what?**

Me: *The VIN? It's the serial number of vehicle.*

Customer: **Oh, uh... how about this? [Reads 8 numbers]**

Me: *Okay, that VIN is for a 2007 van.*

Customer: **Oh, so you need the one off my car?**

Me: *Yes. Of course.*

Customer: **Well I'm going to have to call you back with that. [Hangs up]**

Me: *Hello, Parts.*

Customer: Hi Parts, I'm putting a sliding rear window into a vehicle that doesn't have one. What kind of harnesses do I need?

Me: *... Wait... what?*

Customer: I need the part numbers for the harnesses that I'm going to need.

Me: *Harnesses for a sliding rear window?*

Customer: Yeah, there's a kit.

Me: *Okay. What sort of vehicle are you adding this sliding rear window to?*

Customer: Well, it's a Ford van, but they told me that you had the kit I needed.

Me: *... Someone told you that we have a kit to add a sliding rear window to a Ford van? That's not a thing. We don't have parts for Fords here.*

Customer: Ugh, is there someone else I can talk to? Someone who actually knows what they're doing?

Me: *Yeah... no. I'm the only person here today. I really think a Ford dealership is going to be your best bet.*

Customer: You're completely useless!

Me: *Well, I try my hardest. [Hangs up]*

Me: *Hello, Parts.*

Customer: **The news says it's going to snow, and I need to get the front replaced.**

Me: *... Uh, alright... Would you happen to have your VIN handy?*

Customer: **No, that's upstairs. Can't you just give me a ballpark price?**

Me: *...A ballpark price for what exactly?*

Customer: **For what it costs to replace the front!**

Me: *Let me get you to Service, hopefully they'll have some information for you.*

Customer: **I just talked to them! They didn't know what I was talking about, and said I had to talk to you!**

Me: *... Well, I guess we're in the same boat. I'm really going to need more information.*

Customer: **This is all I ever get when I call you people! [Hangs up]**

[And why do you think that might be?]

Me: *Hello, Parts.*

Customer: **I need that symbol on the front.**

Me: *Okay... Which symbol are we talking about, and what sort of car is it for?*

Customer: **It's red.**

Me: *That's delightful, but I really need to know what sort of car it's for.*

Customer: **It's just that symbol up on the front.**

Me: *Yes. We've established that. But in order for me to look it up, I need to know what sort of car it's for.*

Customer: **Oh, uh... well it's out in the driveway.**

Me: *... Excellent. Do you think you could go have a look and maybe call me back?*

Customer: **I need to do all that just for a symbol?**

Me: *Yes. There's no way for me to look this up without you telling me what sort of car you have.*

Customer: **I'm gonna have to call you back. [Hangs up]**

[Midway through a conversation]

Me: *It looks like I have that in stock, it's about $25 with tax.*

Customer: **Alright, I'm gonna come up there and get one, but I need to take my fiancée to the bathroom first... she always needs the damn bathroom.**

Me: *... Uh... Alright... We'll hold this at the counter for you.*

Customer: **Thanks, it might be a while. [Hangs up]**

[Thanks for the heads-up... I guess?]

Me: *Hello, Parts.*

Customer: **I need to get some touch up paint for my car.**

Me: *Alright, what kind of car do you have?*

Customer: **It's a '91 Deville.**

Me: [Gets VIN info] *That paint is about $25, and it'll take 3 - 5 business days to get in.*

Customer: **Man! That's cheap! And that'll cover the whole car?! The body shop said it was going to cost like $3000.**

Me: *Uhhh... No. This is a touch up tube. It's about a half ounce of paint.*

Customer: **Oh. So... how many of those do I need to repaint my car?**

Me: *Well, these things are about the size of a jar of nail polish... so, probably a few hundred? I honestly have no idea.*

Customer: **... Oh... so I wouldn't save any money doing it this way.**

Me: *No... The body shop would be your best bet.*

Me: *Hello, Parts.*

Customer: **Hi, I lost both my sets of keys last night, and you all need to make me a new one.**

Me: *Well, before I can do anything, you're going to have to supply me with proof of ownership of the vehicle. I'm going to need the title of the vehicle, the registration, and a valid driver's license, all documents must reflect the same name and address.*

Customer: **Alright, I got all of that.**

Me: *Excellent. What kind of vehicle is this for?*

Customer: **Well, actually, I don't have the registration. I do have an insurance card for my other car, though. Also, the title is in a different name, and it doesn't have my address on it. And I got a state ID.**

Me: *So... actually you have literally nothing that proves you own this vehicle.*

Customer: **Why do I have to prove I own it?! I just need you to make me a key for it.**

[I feel like I gave the key speech about a million times... and it was listened to maybe twice.]

[First call of Saturday morning]

Me:	*Hello, Parts.*

Customer: **Yeah, Hello Parts, I've got a '97 Chevy Corbin, and I need to know something.**

Me: *You have a '97... Corbin?*

Customer: **Yeah, the four door one. I need to know if you have to take the whole dash out to replace the turn signal.**

Me: *... If you have to take the... dash out? To replace a turn signal? Would you happen to have the last 8 digits of the VIN for this... '97 Corbin?*

Customer: **Oh... I'll have to call you back with that.
[Hangs up]**

[Two minutes later... Phone rings]

Me: *Hello, Parts.*

Customer: **Yeah, I got those 8 digits, it's 3 8 7 4 1 5 6 9 8 2 5 6 3 4 5 2 1...**

Me: *Whoa. Hang on. I just need the last 8 digits.*

Customer: **Hang on a second... [Reads 8 random numbers]**

Me: *Alright, that's not coming up as a valid VIN.*

Customer: **Alright, hang on. I'll call you right back.
[Hangs up]**

[Two minutes later... Phone rings]

Me: *... Hello... Parts.*

Customer: **Alright, try these numbers**
               [Reads another random string of numbers]

Me: *Alright, that's coming up as an '03 Avalanche.*
               What sort of vehicle did you say this was again?

Customer: **Man, it's not an Avalanche, it's a '97 Corbins.**

Me: *Well, see, I'm just confused, because we've never*
               made a car called a Corbins.

Customer: **Well, I'm looking at it right now, and it's a...**
               C... o... b... a... l... t...

Me: *So... it's a Cobalt?*

Customer: **Yeah, it's a '97 Cobalt.**

Me: *Alright... Chevrolet didn't start making the Cobalt*
               until 2005... are we sure we have correct
               information? If you're by the car, could you just
               read me the VIN off it?

Customer: **You know what, I'll just do this some other**
               time. [Hangs up]

Me: *Hello, Parts.*

Customer: **Is this Parts?**

Me: *Yes, this is Parts.*

Customer: **Alright Parts, I need to ask you something. See, my car starts, and it runs just fine, but it won't move.**

Me: *Okay.*

Customer: **So what part is that?**

Me: *Pardon me?*

Customer: **What part do I need to make my car move again?**

Me: *I'm sorry, there's just no way I can diagnose something like this over the phone. Your best bet would be to have a technician look at it.*

Customer: **This is Parts, right?**

Me: *It certainly is.*

Customer: **And you can't tell me what part I need to fix my car?!**

Me: *No, I'm sorry, diagnosis is handled by the Service Department.*

Customer: **Alright, let me ask you another question.**

Me: *Okay.*

Customer: **A part of my car is broken, right?**

Me: *Evidently.*

Customer: **And you work in Parts, right??**

Me: *Yes. Again, diagnosing problems, particularly one as vague as this, is handled by Service. You need to have the car looked at by a technician, this way, you'll get it fixed properly the first time.*

Customer: **I want to talk to your manager.**

Me: *I'm sure he'd love to hear from you. He'll be in Monday at 8 AM.*

Customer: **[Hangs up]**

[Did we figure out what day of the week this was?]

Me: *Hello, Parts.*

Customer: **How much is my muffler?**

Me: *I don't know, what sort of car do you have?*

Customer: **I think it's an '09 Traverse.**

Me: *Would you happen to have the last 8 of your VIN?*

Customer: **Nope.**

Me: *Alright, is it single or dual?*

Customer: **Dual.**

Me: *Looks like you'd be around $1200 for a new muffler.*

Customer: **Oh, well the muffler shop said it was $150, so you have to match that.**

Me: *Nope.*

Customer: **... Oh... [Hangs up]**

[Oh, you said the magic words, let me give you 90% off.]

Me: *Hello, Parts.*

Customer: **I'm calling about weatherstrips.**

Me: *Okay...*

Customer: **So are you going to tell me how much they cost?!**

Me: *Well, I at least need to know what kind of car you have.*

Customer: **Oh my god, I already told you all this.**

Me: *No, sir, you haven't; that's why I asked.*

Customer: **So you're not going to tell me what they cost?!**

Me: *I just need to know what ki...*

Customer: **[Hangs up]**

Me: *Hello, Parts.*

Customer: **You got sun visors in stock?**

Me: *Maybe, it kinda depends on what sort of car you have.*

Customer: **Well, could you go look? I need two.**

Me: *Alright... Well, what sort of car do you have?*

Customer: **I've got an '06 Impala.**

Me: *And you're looking for both sun visors?*

Customer: **No, man, the visors are for my sister's car.**

Me: *Okay... and what sort of car does your sister have?*

Customer: **Uh... I dunno, should I have her call you?**

Me: *That would probably be a good idea.*

Me: *Hello, Parts.*

Customer: **Yeah, I've got a '89 postal truck.**

Me: *...Alright.*

Customer: **It's got a diesel.**

Me: *Excellent. What sort of part are you looking for?*

Customer: **I just need that tube.**

Me: *...And which tube might that be.*

Customer: **It's *that* tube. Right *there*.**

Me: *... Right where?*

Customer: **Right *there*. I'm looking at it right now.**

Me: *Okay... well, we're on the phone... I can't see what you're looking at.*

Customer: **Well then how are you going to get me the right pipe?**

[I don't know, man...]

285

[...]

"You would be named Hollywood, with your hair all standing up like that."

"Hi, I have an Avalanche, and there's three things on it, and someone stole one, and I need to know how much that is."

"That part in the middle, it works fine, but it doesn't turn red unless I put it in reverse. Do you have one of those?"

"I'm not going to end up in the book, am I?"

[I did wear a particularly odd hairstyle the whole time I worked there.]

[Chapter 12]

Saturdays...

[Ask anyone in this field... there's just something about Saturdays...]

[Salesman walks up to the counter]

Salesman: **My customer's mom ordered a key.**

Me: *... ... Okay.*

Salesman: **Oh, is that not enough information?**

Me: *Do you have a name for me? Or a stock number? Or literally anything for me to go on?*

Salesman: **Oh, uh... no, I don't have any of that.**

Me: *Well, then it's going to be a bit difficult to figure out what's on order, don't you think?*

Salesman: **Uh... I'll go find that out.**

Me: *I'll be eagerly waiting for you...*

[Feel free to take your time, it's not like I'm busy... being the only person in the department, covering the phones and both counters...]

Me: *Hello, Parts.*

Customer: **Someone stole the fancy radio out of my car, so I'm putting the factory one back in and I need to get the code to unlock my radio.**

Me: *Is the radio in the car?*

Customer: **Yeah, it's in the car.**

Me: *Alright... Well, with the car on, but not started, hold down presets 2 and 3 and a set of numbers should show up.*

Customer: **It's not doing anything.**

Me: *Does it say anything on the radio currently?*

Customer: **It's not even lighting up.**

Me: *... But it's in the car and hooked up and everything?*

Customer: **Oh, no, it's just sitting in my lap.**

Me: *... ...Alright. You're going to have to actually hook it up in order to unlock it.*

Customer: **Oh, well then I'll have to call you back.**

[I mean... he was technically correct... the radio was IN the car...]

Me: *Hello, Parts.*

Customer: **I want to speak to Phillip.**

Me: *Phil isn't in today. He'll be back in at 8 on Monday.*

Customer: **He'll be in on Monday? Okay, well you can help me.**

Me: *Alright, excellent, how can I help?*

Customer: **I need to speak to Phillip.**

Me: *I understand that, but he's not here today. If you need to talk to him, he'll be in at 8 on Monday.*

Customer: **Ohhhh, he'll be in on Monday?**

Me: *Yes. He'll be in at 8 AM.*

Customer: **Well you should be able to help me.**

Me: *Wonderful. Excellent. What sort of car do you have?*

Customer: **Well, Phillip has all of that information. Can I speak to him?**

Me: *Yes. You can. When you call back on Monday, after 8 AM.*

Customer: **Ohhh, he'll be there on Monday? I'll call him back then.**

[Dude, Phil isn't Beetlejuice. You don't just say his name a bunch of times and he magically appears.]

Me: *Hello, Parts.*

Customer: **Yes, do you have a Saturn Ion?**

Me: *The actual car? No. We don't sell Saturns.*

Customer: **Well, I was told to call the dealership if I needed an Ion! Are you telling me you don't have one?!**

Me: *Correct. Saturn has been out of business for over 2 years, and they haven't made the Ion in nearly 7.*

Customer: **Well, you tell me what I'm supposed to do then!**

[Is "go away" an option?]

Me: *Hello, Parts.*

Customer: **Yeah, does my SS Trailblazer have single or double exhaust?**

Me: *Uh... I don't know. You tell me. Do you have one exhaust pipe or two?*

Customer: **The hell do you mean 'you tell me'? I just asked you!**

Me: *Okay... All of the SS Trailblazers come with single exhaust from the factory. So, I have to assume, unless you've changed it, you have single exhaust.*

Customer: **Oh yeah?! Well then how come I see them with double exhaust all the time?!**

Me: *Presumably because they added dual exhaust after they were purchased.*

Customer: **Man, fuck you. You don't know what you're talking about. [Hangs Up]**

[First call of Saturday morning]

Me: *Hello, Parts.*

Customer: **I got the last 5 digits of my VIN, and I need that plastic molding on the door; the one that holds the radiator in place.**

Me: *Well, first off, I'm going to need your last 8 digits... and you're looking for a molding on the door that... holds your radiator in place? I'm pretty sure that's not a thing.*

Customer: **If it's not a thing, then how come I need one?**

Me: *I couldn't begin to imagine, but I assure you there are no moldings on your doors that hold your radiator in place.*

Customer: **It's too early in the morning for this.**

Me: *At least we can both agree on that.*

Customer: **[Hangs Up]**

Me: *Hello, Parts.*

Customer: **I'm just calling to see if the order for [name] is in.**

Me: *Yes. You spoke to me 5 minutes ago, and I told you it was here.*

Customer: **I did?**

Me: *You did.*

Customer: **I don't think I did.**

Me: *Do you drive an '07 Buick Rendezvous?*

Customer: **Yeah, I do.**

Me: *Okay, then yes, you just called 5 minutes ago, and I told you your parts were in.*

Customer: **Oh, well I don't remember any of that.**

[If you didn't just call me, I really need to get some credit for guessing that car.]

[At the counter]

Me: *Hi, is there something I can help you with?*

Customer: **I need to pick up that sensor.**

Me: *Alright, what sensor are we looking for?*

Customer: **It's a... uh... tire sensor.**

Me: *For what kind of car?*

Customer: **He said it's an... uh... '06 Lucerne. It's under Eric Clark. Vince said you would have one out for me.**

Me: *Alright, well, there's no one named Vince here, and I don't have anything held for an Eric Clark... and the '06 Lucerne didn't have tire pressure sensors.*

Customer: **Let me call him. [Gets on the phone] Yeah man, I'm down here at [different dealership] and they say they don't know anything about it.**

Me: *You're at the wrong dealership.*

Customer: **[To me] No I'm not.**

Me: *Sir, I know where I work. If this was that dealership, why am I wearing a monogrammed shirt with a different dealership's name on it?*

Customer: **[To phone] Hey, where's [other dealership] at? [Walks away]**

Me: *Hello, Parts.*

Customer: **I need to get a key for a Ford.**

Me: *Then you're going to have to call a Ford dealership.*

Customer: **Can't you call them for me?**

Me: *No. But I'll gladly sell you all of the GM keys that you would like.*

Customer: **So you're really not going to call them for me?**

Me: *No. If you need a key for a Ford the you are going to have to call them yourself.*

Customer: **Man, you all are supposed to help me! [Hangs up]**

[Gonna need you to put on your big boy pants here. If you were capable of calling me, you're capable of calling Ford and handling this yourself.]

Me: *Hello, Parts.*

Customer: **Yeah... who are those guys at those desks?**

Me: *Pardon me?*

Customer: **I need one of those guys at those desks.**

Me: *You need... a... salesman?*

Customer: **Nah, not one of them, one of those other guys.**

Me: *At desks?*

Customer: **Yeah... by where they fix the cars.**

Me: *A Service Writer? One second, I'll transfer you.*

["Guys at Desks" is the name of our Service Writers' barbershop quartet.]

[First call of Saturday morning]

Me: *Hello, Parts.*

Customer: **Hello. I have a Chevy and I need to replace all of the sensors.**

Me: *... Okay. What sort of Chevy do you have? And which sensor are we looking for?*

Customer: **ALL OF THEM!**

Me: *I promise you, you don't need to replace ALL of your sensors. What's wrong with your car?*

Customer: **YES I DO! I NEED ALL OF THE SENSORS! THERE'S A LIGHT BLINKING ON MY DASHBOARD!**

Me: *I'm going to transfer you to Service, and hopefully they'll be able to help you out.*

Customer: **[Hangs Up]**

[You can ignore the check engine light, but the replace all sensors light is the real deal.]

[First call of... yet another... Saturday morning]

Me: *Hello, Parts.*

Customer: **Yeah, I put a new engine in my car, and I need a dipstick for it. You got one?**

Me: *I don't know, maybe. I'm going to need a bit more information to look that up.*

Customer: **Well then you suck at your job! [Hangs up]**

[Man, if you think I suck at this, you're really lucky you didn't talk to anyone else in this department...]

[Open the counter Saturday morning]

Me: *Hi... can I help you with something?*

Customer: **Yeah, I need you to sell me something to make my car faster.**

Me: *Well, unfortunately, we only sell original equipment, so if it's anything that your car didn't come with from the factory, we're not going to have it.*

Customer: **Well... sell me one with more numbers on it.**

Me: *... What? ... More... numbers?*

Customer: **Yeah, mine only goes up to 120, but some of those other ones go to 150.**

Me: *Are you... talking about a gauge cluster? You want a different gauge cluster with... more numbers on it?*

Customer: **Yeah man, so then my car can go to 150.**

Me: *That's not... cars don't work like that. That's not a thing that you can do.*

Customer: **So you aren't going to help me?**

Me: *No... I'm sorry. There's just nothing I can do here.*

Customer: **[Walks away]**

[This guy clearly attended the Nigel Tufnel school of car tuning.]

[At the counter... on a Saturday]

Me: *Hi, is there something I can help you with?*

Customer: **I need a part, and I've got the part number.**

Me: *Well that's easy. What number do you have?*

Customer: **[Reads number off a piece of paper]**

Me: *Unfortunately, it doesn't look like I stock this, and my locator is saying that it's actually been discontinued. I don't see any stock anywhere in the country.*

Customer: **Well, I was just at a different dealership and they said you had one. They gave me this printout.**

Me: *[Looks at printout] This does say that we have that part, but the date at the top looks like this was from over two years ago. When did you get this?*

Customer: **Well it felt like it was just the other day.**

Me: *I understand, but if you had come here two years ago, we probably would have had it... but I can't get this part anymore...*

Customer: **Alright then. [Walks away]**

[On... a Saturday...]

Me: *Hello, Parts.*

Customer: **I need to buy some parts for my car.**

Me: *Alright, what kind of car do you have, and what parts are you looking for?*

Customer: **I'm parked in your parking lot.**

Me: *Well, if you'd like to come inside to the Parts Deparment, I'd be glad to assist you. We're right next to the cashier.*

Customer: **NO! I'm not coming inside! You need to come out here and help me! I don't want to have to get out of my car!**

Me: *Unfortunately, I'm the only one here today, and I'll need my computers in order to look up any parts. If you'd like to come inside, I'll gladly assist you, but I can't leave the department.*

Customer: **Well fuck you then! [Hangs up]**

[2 minutes later. Someone is pounding on the Retail Counter]

Me: *Hi. Please don't do that. Can I help you with something?*

Customer: **I SAID I WANTED YOU TO COME OUT TO MY CAR AND HELP ME!**

Me: *You also said you weren't going to come inside. But now that you have, can I help you with something?*

Customer: **THAT'S FUCKING IT! I'M GETTING YOU FIRED!**

Me: *That's fine. Honestly, you'd be doing me a favor.*

Customer: **GET YOUR FUCKING MANAGER OUT HERE!**

Me: *He'll be in 8 on Monday, and I'm sure he'd love to hear from you.*

Customer: **[Stomps away]**

[Nothing makes an angry person angrier than not returning that anger toward them.]

[A Single Moment of Positivity]

There never was much gratitude coming across the counter in Parts (if that hasn't been made abundantly clear in the preceding pages). When most people approached the counter, they were already not in a great mood, because something has gone wrong with their vehicle, and dealerships have earned a — what's a polite way to say this — *certain* reputation. Most days, it felt like no matter what level of positivity you tried to bring to any interaction, you would, at best, be met with disinterested ambivalence, or, at worst... well, just flip back one page to get an idea.

In all my time at the counter, there's been one interaction that has stuck out as potentially the only time that I walked away from a customer and felt genuinely good about everything that had happened.

A gentleman walked up to the counter, and I greeted him with my usual, "Hi, is there something I can help you with?" He pointed to his ear and shook his head; he was deaf. My stomach sank involuntarily, because this was difficult enough when people could hear what I was saying (of course, whether or not they actually listened was another story), but it wasn't going to stop me from trying.

He handed me a piece of paper with a VIN and 5 - 6 transmission parts written on it; real internal stuff; the sorts of things that I would usually have a tech calling out specific numbers on diagrams to get right. He had a bit of trepidation on his face, but I just shrugged and smiled, and started opening transmission diagrams.

We spent nearly 20 minutes at it. There was a line of customers behind him; the phones were ringing; the techs were at the counter; and it didn't matter, because we were just having a great time. There was no yelling, there were no threats, it was just two goofy dudes pointing at things on a screen and making different faces at each other.

When I eventually brought him his parts, he just signed "thank you" over and over. Not knowing any actual sign language, I just gave him the biggest thumbs-up I could, and he reached out and grabbed my thumb and practically shook my whole arm. I wish all of my customers were that guy.

[Changelog]

V1.1 -

P. 32 - Changed both instances of "Infinity" to "Infiniti."
P. 292 - Line 12, adjusted indent.

V 1.2 -

P. 116 - Line 3, fixed text formatting.

[The end.]

Made in the USA
Middletown, DE
13 August 2023

36623553R00182